# Unlocking Lean Six Sigma

## A Competency-Based Approach to Applying Continuous Process Improvement Principles and Best Practices

*If I had an hour to solve a problem, I'd spend 55 minutes thinking about the problem and 5 minutes about the solution.*

– Albert Einstein

# Unlocking Lean Six Sigma

A Competency-Based Approach to Applying Continuous Process Improvement Principles and Best Practices

*A practical guidebook for professional development, and includes Centrestar's **Knowledge Review Test***

First Edition 2021

ISBN: 978-0-578-87369-5

Centrestar Learning

State College, Pennsylvania, USA

**www.centrestar.com**

# Unlocking Lean Six Sigma

**Endorsement for Dr. Wesley Donahue's Unlocking Lean Six Sigma**

"The simple process examples conveyed in this book demonstrate that you don't need to be an engineer to apply Lean Six Sigma tools to your job. The tools can be applied in any organization or industry. This book is the best Lean Sigma guide available. It is written in plain English and extremely easy to understand. Most Definitely RECOMMENDED! Well Done!"

**– Dr. Jong Gyu Park,**
Assistant Professor of Management, Penn State University

"Unlocking Lean Six Sigma is an excellent tool for all types of learners to develop skills in process improvement. Its variety of content provides the reader with a well-rounded foundation for professional success. As a former student of Dr. Donahue, I was able to leverage the skillset outlined in this guide during my engineering career through operational development and kaizen events. I highly recommend this guidebook to anyone looking to further develop process improvement skills or become certified in Lean Six Sigma."

**– Joseph Vais,**
Engineer, Volvo Group Trucks Technology

"In this turbulent time successful organizations are able to stay focused on the key processes that drive their success. Wes has built a resource that will help leaders at all levels to understand how they can use Lean and Six Sigma to improve the efficiency and effectiveness of their organization. The competency framework provides the reader with tools they can use to guide their own learning and facilitate the learning of other team members. This is a book you will keep on your desk not gathering dust on your bookshelf."

**– John E. Park,**
D.Ed., Director, Leadership Development & Management Consulting,
Baker Tilly Virchow Krause, LLPl

"Dr. Donahue's book helps students and working professionals understand the fundamentals and implementation insights for Lean Six Sigma. For individuals who are curious about process improvement initiatives, this book provides valuable insights, how to's and technical knowledge and tools to get started. The book also provides the option of registering and completing Lean Sigma Yellow Belt credential through Centrestar. This certificate is now highlighted on my resume!"

**– Sagun Giri**,
PhD Candidate, College of Ed, Penn State University

"Professor Donahue has put together a comprehensive yet simple to use resource for individuals wanting to hone their process improvement skills. Aspiring young professionals will find his book invaluable."

**– Kartik Singhal**,
Operations Engineer - Supply Chain Strategy & Planning, Cummins Inc.

"Lean sigma has been around for a while but it is still a challenge for organizations, process teams, and individuals. Dr. Donahue uses his business and teaching experience to provide practical instruction that helps you master this powerful business approach. Here, you select your own problem then learn and apply the lean sigma tools in a step-by-step manner from the beginning to the end of your project. From my point of view, that is the best type of instruction you can get!"

**– Patrick Knobloch**,
President, Innate Management, Inc.

"The Lean Six Sigma principles you'll learn by using this guide will give you the tools and the processes you need to know how to analyze work process problems and to develop lasting solutions to address the root causes of annoying problems. The outcomes achieved by practicing the prescribed approaches will earn you the recognition as a problem-solving leader and a facilitator of excellence, someone your peers and managers look to when things aren't going as they should. What you learn from this book will easily transfer among industries, may be applied in organizations where you work or volunteer, and will even improve your personal and home life. "

**– Dr. Eric Bergstrom**,
Assistant Professor, Lean Sigma Instructor, Penn State University

# Unlocking Lean Six Sigma

A Competency-Based Approach to Applying Continuous Process Improvement Principles and Best Practices

*If you can't describe what you are doing as a process,*
*you don't know what you are doing.*

– William Edward Deming

## Preface

For the past thirty years, I have helped organizations large and small build leadership competence, work as teams, and focus on priorities. As an engineer transplanted into the educational field, my role has been to help organizations improve their performance.

While organizations think they are unique, I have learned they have three common challenges: 1) improve internal and external communications, 2) work collaboratively as a team, and 3) identify and focus efforts and resources on their most important priorities. This last item, the need to identify and focus on the most important priorities, is at the heart of this book.

I have worked with business clients in almost every type of industry and organization, and one truth holds: "organizations either get better, or they get worse," and the choice is theirs. As an organization development practitioner, I subscribe to the philosophy that the people doing the work know best what it takes to improve the associated work processes. And, on average, consensus improvement decision-making will yield the best results. That said, I have watched organizations embrace various improvement approaches, including Quality Circles, Total Quality Management (TQM), Lean, Six Sigma, and others with mixed success. Some people might say that these approaches are "faddish "or the "flavor of the month." I will tell you that if you want to improve continuously, the tools common to these approaches are invaluable, and knowing how to apply them are crucial to your success.

No matter which improvement approach you choose, it involves some sort of problem-solving process: identifying and describing an issue, analyzing the situation, generating alternatives, implementing the best alternative, and reporting and controlling the results. In my experience, too many organizations get hung-up and overcomplicate their improvement approaches. They don't focus on the "low-hanging fruit" or improvement opportunities in front of them.

Simple is good, and with this philosophy in mind, I have tried to blend the improvement approaches and focus on several simple process examples to demonstrate the use of the common tools. The term Lean Sigma and Lean Six Sigma are often used synonymously to refer to this blended approach. However, in a jargon-crowded field, words like Lean and Six Sigma can be intimidating for both beginners and experienced users. Don't worry, this book is written in plain language and packed with simple straight-forward examples. This easy-to-follow guide provides you with tools and techniques for implementing Lean Six Sigma and managing process improvement initiatives in your organization.

In Lean Six Sigma courses that I teach, I ask participants to apply what they learn by first selecting a simple work-related process they find problematic, then follow along throughout the book and use it as a guide to apply the tools to their work process.

The choice is yours: Choose to improve!

Dr. Wesley E. Donahue

2021

# Acknowledgments

I did not create this book alone, and I want to acknowledge the people who contributed significantly to the work: Drs. Lisa and Alyssa Donahue and Marc Donahue for their invaluable research efforts in tracking down articles, books, and other sources needed for identifying examples; Dr. Eric Bergstrom and Patrick Knobloch for their content expertise; Richard Tunaley and Billie Tomlinson for their editing and attention to detail; Valentine Platon for adding graphics that help bring the text to life; Alex Donahue for thoughtful design consultation; former instructors and professional associates at Penn State Management who shared their business and industry wisdom and years of teaching experience; the individuals who took the time to review the manuscript; and the many thousands of people who participated in improvement projects, without whom this book would lack the richness of real-world detail. To all these people, I offer a sincere and heartfelt Thank you!

# Contents

*If you define the problem correctly, you almost have the solution.*

– Steve Jobs

# Introduction

*Continuous improvement is better than delayed perfection.*

– Mark Twain

# Welcome

Are you looking for ways to improve the work processes in your organization? Do you want to improve your skills to increase your presence in your organization? If so, you have come to the right place.

This guide combines the principles, best practices, and tools of Lean and Six Sigma methodologies into an easy to understand system and presents the information in a unique competency-based approach so you can immediately apply what you learn. This approach has helped thousands of people achieve success. It will help you too.

# Audience

This is a practical guide for people who want to advance their professional skills and have their coworkers and managers view them as effective contributors, and people who want rewarding careers.

The guide is aimed at young professionals, people taking on fresh challenges or moving into new careers, and anyone who wants to learn process skills needed by every organization. In effect, this guide is a valuable resource for anyone in today's workplace.

The guide includes a 120-question Knowledge Review Test that you can use to self-test your understanding of the material and how you apply it in your workplace.

People interested in earning professional development hours have the option of earning 12 hours by studying the guide and formally taking the Knowledge Review Test through Centrestar. For more information, see the Earn PDHs and a Lean Sigma Yellow Belt Credential section in the guide.

For more information about earning professional development hours, visit us at www.centrestar.com. We are also on Facebook.

# Purpose

The guide introduces you to continuous process improvement in organizational settings and describes how to apply Lean and Six Sigma methodologies. It gives you what you need to know so that you can apply these time-proven principles, best practices, and tools in your work.

Continuous process improvement initiatives are often untaken in projects, and so the guide also touches on project management. Topics include how to find problems, describe current work processes, analyze what is happening and why it needs to change, how to identify, plan, and implement improvements, and how to report information to others.

If you are not familiar with the terms, Lean and Six Sigma are formal methodologies. If you search online, you will find many references to these terms. Some may cause you to think the methodologies are complex. Indeed, people sometimes think a steep learning curve is necessary to use them effectively. But this is not the case.

This guide gives you a *practical* approach to making the tools work for you in your work environment. While there is always more to learn, for example, more to learn about the statistical methods used in Six Sigma, you do not need to understand all the technical details or be a mathematician to make good use of the methodologies. You can also continue learning as you gain real-world experience.

While Lean and Six Sigma are different, and you can read about the differences and commonalities in Concept 2, we do not distinguish between them except when addressing specific methods. Both Lean and Six Sigma are used in improvement projects, and they have much in common. They both help you better define, measure, analyze, control, and improve work processes. Our focus is on how you can apply the tools common to both methodologies, and we simply refer to the combined principles and practices as Lean Six Sigma.

## Organization

The guide begins with a Getting Started section. It introduces our competency-based approach and the main competencies associated with continuous process improvement. Our competency-based approach stresses that having a competency is not *thinking* you know something. Competency means you can *behave* in ways that demonstrate your skills to the people you work with and your customers or clients.

Getting Started wraps up with a few self-review questions for you to assess where you are now and what you want to learn more about as you go through the guide.

The guide is organized into ten key Concepts, with the first being an introduction to Lean and Six Sigma. It describes what they have in common and how they differ, and how they relate to the project management life cycle.

Each Concept after the first describes a specific skill involved in Lean Sigma continuous process improvement. For example, Concept 3 describes how to observe a work process. The guide also has many worksheets with examples of how to use them.

Near the end of each Concept, you will find a process improvement case studies that illustrate the information presented. After that, you will see reminders of the key points you have learned.

You will then find an Enhance Your Learning section. It provides several additional resources for you to review and learn from, for example, videos and websites that offer specialized information.

Finally, at the end of each Concept, you will find a Reinforce Your Leaning section that directs your attention to you and your job. You will complete questions to help you consider and self-test what you learned and how well you can apply the information.

## How to Use This Guide

We structured the guide to be hands-on with options for how you use the material. The guide supplies the knowledge and practical steps you will need to improve your skills in any of the Concepts you select. You will need to provide the grit.

One way to use the guide is to read it straight through. If you are new to the idea of continuous improvement, we suggest you do that, at least for a first read-through. After that, you can tackle any of the individual Concepts. Or you can jump immediately to specific Concepts depending on your interests and goals.

We recommend you start by reviewing the table of contents so you understand the organization. Read the Getting Started section, and then take the introductory assessment by rating your level of agreement with the ten statements. This will help you clarify your current thinking.

After that, you might scan the guide. Scanning will help you pinpoint areas where you may have an information gap and areas where you feel confident. From there, you can set your learning goals and dive deeper into the material, and tackle topics that are currently problematic or frustrating to you.

At the end of the guide is a Recap Checklist. It lists all the 30 What to Do actions from each Concept in the guide. You can use the Recap to test how well you remember the key points.

To learn and grow, you must engage fully with the material as it applies to you and your job. Ask yourself questions as you read the material. Do the activities and answer the questions in each Concept. Make notes. Look for ideas new to you and consider how they fit with your current knowledge. Recognize what you already know and can build on, and what might be a new way of looking at something.

As with most things in life, you will get out of this guide what you put into it. As mentioned in the Preface, one of the best ways to learn is to select a simple work-related process you find problematic, and then use that process as you work through the material. This "working on a real problem" approach is one of the best ways to learn.

## Use as a Text or Workshop Guide

We designed this book primarily for individuals; however, faculty teaching at universities and colleges will also find the book to be invaluable. This book can be used as a supplemental text for credit courses, supplementary guide for process improvement teams, or as a workbook for seminars, workshops, and learn-at-lunch programs.

For instrustors, the following teaching resources are available:

- Powerpoint slides with instructor notes
- Teaching/learning case scenarios
- Web links to learning resources
- Workshop timelines
- Multiple choice questions, organized by key concept for use as assessments
- Answers to practice test questions

# Getting Started

*The most dangerous kind of waste is the waste we do not recognize.*

– Shigeo Shingo

This guide combines the principles and best practices of **Lean** and **Six Sigma** methodologies and shows you how to use these tools for work process improvements in your organization. Our focus is to provide straightforward and practical information you can apply in your projects and initiatives.

While Lean and Six Sigma concepts have their roots in manufacturing, studies show that people have achieved similar results in financial services, healthcare, and government projects and initiatives. For example, the US National Library of Medicine, National Center for Biotechnical Information reported in a longitudinal study of several healthcare processes aimed at improving efficiency in a catheterization laboratory that significant improvements were made in areas such as turn-time, physician downtime, and on-time patient arrival (Elsevier, Inc. 2016).

Likewise, through the use of Lean Six Sigma, government agencies and academic institutions which are prone to developing overly complex and inefficient processes have been able to achieve dramatic results. As an example, one government agency was able to dramatically cut the cycle time required to obtain security clearances, saving time, money, and frustration. In another example, many universities have been able to streamline their admissions process by eliminating unnecessary process steps and unnecessary processes, resulting in the early identifications for top recruits and weeding out of unqualified candidates.

Other examples common in manufacturing, government, and the military are improvement of procurement and preventative maintenance processes. In business, common examples focus on improvement of new product development processes and, more globally, strategic innovation processes.

In the guide, we focus on how you can apply these tools in your work and simply refer to the combined principles and practices synonymously as Lean Sigma or Lean

Six Sigma. However, you can learn more about the specifics of Lean and Six Sigma and how they are typically used in improvement projects in Concept 2, "Differentiate Lean and Six Sigma Methodologies."

As discussed in the Introduction, the focus of Lean Six Sigma as a **continuous improvement methodology** and **process management strategy** is to **improve processes, eliminate waste, reduce variation**, and **better serve customers**.

By the end of this guide, you will know how to:

- Explain how Lean Six Sigma fits with other continuous improvement initiatives in your organization.

- Evaluate Lean Six Sigma tools and their intended use as related to work process improvement.

- Apply Lean Six Sigma concepts and approaches in practical and real-world applications.

- Solve problems using the A3 methodology, which includes an analysis of the current state and the future state of a process.

- Prepare typical project reports and presentations.

The goal of the guide is to show you how to identify and apply Lean Six Sigma concepts and tools to a process improvement initiative of your choosing. The process you identify could be one you see as problematic and that you believe – given attention – could result in a new or enhanced process closer to an ideal you envision.

## Our Competency Model and Structured Learning

The foundation of our work and this guide is our research-based **Competency Model**. The model, which is rooted in work by the U.S. Department of Labor and others, gives you a framework for structured learning by helping you identify competencies you will need to successfully apply **Lean Six Sigma tools** in your work.

## What is a Competency?

If you ask people to define competency, you may be amazed at the variety of responses you receive.

We define a *competency* as a set of skills, knowledge, attitudes, and behaviors that are observable and measurable. The emphasis here is on *observable* and *measurable*. It is not enough that you *think* you are competent in an area. You must *behave* in ways that demonstrate your competence to others.

## The Centrestar Competency Model

Our framework has 35 competency dimensions associated with successful performance in leadership and professional roles, as illustrated below.

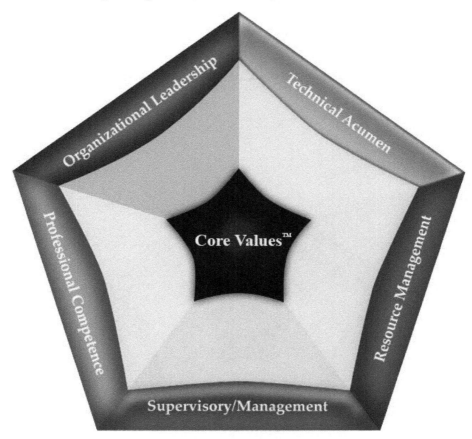

**Centrestar's Competency Model**

Based on thousands of business participant responses from many industries, we clustered the 35 competencies into five competency domains, named and color coded as follows:

    A.  Resource Management – blue

    B.  Professional Competence – brown

    C.  Supervisory/Management – red

    D.  Organizational Leadership – purple

    E.  Technical Acumen – green

# Understand the Competencies Associated with Lean Six Sigma

In our model, the competencies and clusters may sometimes overlap. However, when reviewing professional proficiencies, we identify the three competencies most closely associated with the skills needed to be successful.

This Lean Six Sigma guide focuses on the competency areas of **Resource Management**, **Problem Solving**, and **Job-Specific Competencies**. The content is most closely associated with the blue colored **Resource Management** competency cluster, as shown below.

## Centrestar's Competency Model

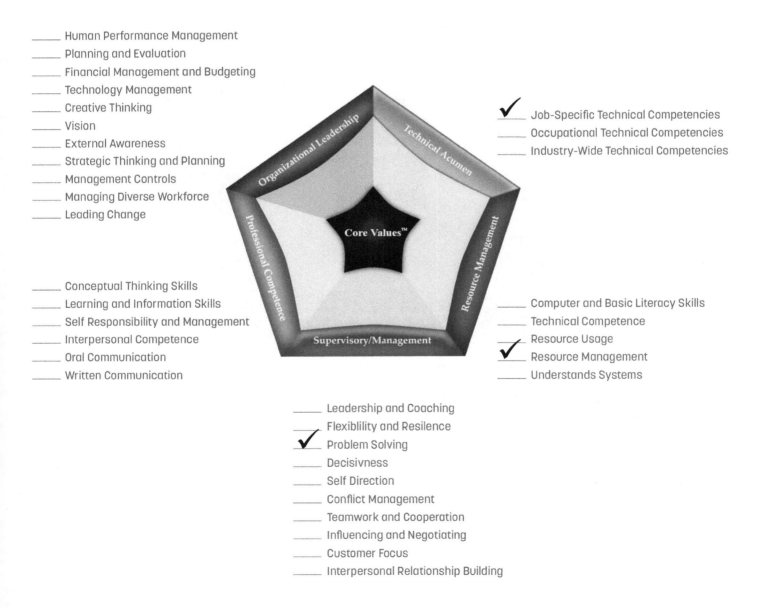

_____ Human Performance Management
_____ Planning and Evaluation
_____ Financial Management and Budgeting
_____ Technology Management
_____ Creative Thinking
_____ Vision
_____ External Awareness
_____ Strategic Thinking and Planning
_____ Management Controls
_____ Managing Diverse Workforce
_____ Leading Change

✓ Job-Specific Technical Competencies
_____ Occupational Technical Competencies
_____ Industry-Wide Technical Competencies

_____ Conceptual Thinking Skills
_____ Learning and Information Skills
_____ Self Responsibility and Management
_____ Interpersonal Competence
_____ Oral Communication
_____ Written Communication

_____ Computer and Basic Literacy Skills
_____ Technical Competence
_____ Resource Usage
✓ Resource Management
_____ Understands Systems

_____ Leadership and Coaching
_____ Flexiblility and Resilence
✓ Problem Solving
_____ Decisivness
_____ Self Direction
_____ Conflict Management
_____ Teamwork and Cooperation
_____ Influencing and Negotiating
_____ Customer Focus
_____ Interpersonal Relationship Building

## Build Your Lean Six Sigma Competencies

Each Concept in this guide describes what you need to know to understand a specific aspect of Lean. Then, at the end of each Concept, you will be asked to cement your understanding of what you have read by answering a few questions that direct your attention to your experience and job, and to reviewing supplemental resources.

By working through the Concepts in this guide, you will build the following competencies:

| Resource Management | Problem Solving | Job-Specific Competencies |
|---|---|---|

Learn more about the Lean Six Sigma specifics associated with these competencies in the next Concept. It discusses how Lean Six Sigma activities fit into the project management life cycle.

## Take Your Temperature for Applying Lean Six Sigma

With you and your organization in mind, read each statement carefully. Next to each, write the number from 1 to 10 that indicates your level of agreement with the statement, with **1 being strongly disagree and 10 being strongly agree**.

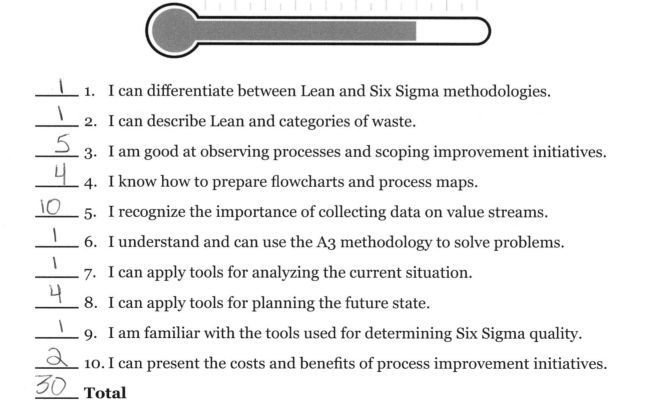

_____1_____  1. I can differentiate between Lean and Six Sigma methodologies.

_____1_____  2. I can describe Lean and categories of waste.

_____5_____  3. I am good at observing processes and scoping improvement initiatives.

_____4_____  4. I know how to prepare flowcharts and process maps.

_____10____  5. I recognize the importance of collecting data on value streams.

_____1_____  6. I understand and can use the A3 methodology to solve problems.

_____1_____  7. I can apply tools for analyzing the current situation.

_____4_____  8. I can apply tools for planning the future state.

_____1_____  9. I am familiar with the tools used for determining Six Sigma quality.

_____2_____  10. I can present the costs and benefits of process improvement initiatives.

_____30____ **Total**

**What problems or situations have you experienced or observed related to process improvement initiatives?**

- The budget and pushback on a P2P system mainly
- Each department in procurement handles things differently than the other, but sometimes that is necessary.
- Process change has been a focus for awhile now so most of the team has been through it and I'm not sure how receptive they'll be to more changes.
- Process changes require many levels of approval and each one needs to be presented in a convincing way.

**Take a few minutes to reflect on your temperature self-assessment related to process improvement methodologies. Then list up to three areas that you would like to develop or improve:**

- Describe Lean and categories of waste.
- A3 methodology and solving problems.
- Apply tools for analyzing the current situation.

As you progress through this guide consider what actions you can take to demonstrate your proficiency in the following competencies and make notes here:

1. **Resource Management**. How can you demonstrate your awareness of technical resources? How can you show you know how to apply resources to achieve desired outcomes?

   - learn the current systems better
   - research the current technology used
   -

2. **Problem Solving**. What can you to show that you can recognize and define problems, analyze relevant information, encourage the development of solutions, and plan to solve problems?

   - understand the process map
   - learn more of the systems currently used
   -

3. **Job-Specific Competencies**. How can you demonstrate the knowledge and skills, and that you know how to use proper methods and procedures, to successfully perform your current job?

   - by suggested process changes
   - knowing the benefits of a P2P system
   - being able to suggest changes even

*Learning is not compulsory; it's voluntary. Improvement is not compulsory; it's voluntary. But to survive, we must learn.*

– W. Edwards Deming

# Differentiate Lean and Six Sigma Methodologies

Here we discuss the essential tools and concepts for better understanding and differentiating **Lean** and **Six Sigma**. Both are **continuous improvement methodologies** regularly referenced separately and together in today's workplace.

Regardless of your position in an organization, waste and defects are of concern to everyone and sooner or later you most likely will be asked to participate in a continuous improvement activity or project. According to the Institute of Quality Assurance, continuous improvement is a gradual, never-ending process of change. Continuous improvement in organizations is driven by competitiveness. Organizations focus on continuous improvement to eliminate wastes of money, people, materials, opportunities, and time. The ideal outcome is that products or services are created through work done less expensively, more efficiently, and more safely.

We use **Lean Sigma** or **Lean Six Sigma** synonymously to describe a **hybrid, continuous improvement methodology** that combines **Lean** and **Six Sigma** concepts, tools, and methodologies to guide organizations through making continuous process improvements. The goals are to assist organizations in improving processes and reducing waste. As appropriate, you can also use **Six Sigma** concepts, tools, and methodologies to better define, measure, analyze, control, and improve processes.

Both methodologies seek to eliminate waste and create the most efficient system possible. However, their approaches to identifying the root cause of waste are not the same.

*Lean* manufacturing or lean production, or often just "lean," is a systematic method for the elimination of waste (Muda) within a process system. Lean considers waste created through overburden (Muri) and waste created through uneven workloads (Mura). Lean typically follows a bottoms-up organizational improvement strategy where goals, projects, and tasks are informed largely by employee feedback.

> **Six Sigma** is a disciplined, data-driven approach and methodology for eliminating variation and defects (driving toward six standard deviations between the mean and the nearest specification limit) in any process, from manufacturing, healthcare, government, to the quality improvement of products or services. Six Sigma typically follows a top-down organizational improvement strategy where goals are passed down the chain of command.

Contemporary Lean thinking has its roots in the Toyota Motor Corporation and the Toyota Production System (TPS). But its origins can be traced to economic thinkers such as Benjamin Franklin who reportedly practiced Lean methodology centuries before it became popular.

Lean is a production practice that considers the expenditure of resources for any goal other than the creation of value for the end customer to be wasteful, and thus a target for elimination. Working from the perspective of the customer who consumes a product or service, value is defined as any action or process that a customer is willing to pay for.

Six Sigma has its foundations in Motorola. However, its methods and philosophies are not limited to manufacturing. They have gained popularity in almost every industry, ranging from healthcare to government.

Six Sigma seeks to improve the quality of process outputs by identifying and removing the causes of defects (errors) and minimizing variability in operations and business processes. It uses a set of quality management methods, including statistical methods, and creates an infrastructure of people within the organization (such as Black Belts, Green Belts, and Yellow Belts) who are experts in these methods. Each Six Sigma project follows a defined sequence of steps and has quantified financial targets (cost reduction and profit increase). The term Sigma has its roots in statistics where the Greek letter "σ" designates the estimated standard deviation or variation for a process output.

Both Lean and Six Sigma focus on leadership and on improving performance results. The Baldrige Framework for Performance Excellence, with its emphasis on both Lean and Six Sigma, describes the criteria used for the Malcolm Baldrige Award. The Malcolm Baldrige Award is the only formal recognition of the performance excellence of both public and private U.S. organizations given by the President of the United States. It is administered by the Baldrige Performance Excellence Program, which is managed by the National Institute of Standards and Technology, an agency of the U.S. Department of Commerce.

Products and services will inherently show some variability when measuring their characteristics. Both Lean Sigma and Six Sigma continuous improvement methodologies seek to eliminate waste and create the most efficient system possible, even though they take different approaches to identifying the root cause of waste.

- **Lean** aims at systematically identifying and eliminating waste throughout an organization. The methods as developed by Toyota consider the expenditure of resources for any goal other than the creation of value for the customer to be wasteful, and thus a target for elimination. This is accomplished by identifying and eliminating nonessential and non-value-added process steps. The goal of implementing Lean Sigma in an organization is to improve process speed, efficiency, quality, and customer satisfaction and loyalty.

- **Six Sigma** was developed by Motorola and is a registered service and trademark of Motorola, Inc. The focus is on improving the quality of products and processes by reducing variation and defects. The method typically follows five steps: define, measure, analyze, improve, and control. The term Sigma in mathematics refers to standard deviation or variance from the mean average. Six Sigma reduces process variation waste by evaluating processes and services using statistical tools. Specifications are typically set for performance with a target of fewer than 3.4 defects per million opportunities.

- **Project Management** is the discipline of planning, organizing, and managing resources to bring about the successful completion of a specific project. The project management cycle typically includes five phases: project initiation, planning, evaluation, controlling, and closing. When we refer to projects in this guide, we are referring to a wide range of activities. For example, a *project* can range from one or two people working to do something in a day or two, or, at the end of the spectrum, a *project* can be a formal work effort with an assigned project manager and where significant work continues over a long period of time.

- **Continuous Improvement and Total Quality Management (TQM)** are comprehensive and overarching philosophies. They affirm that improvement initiatives never end. They incorporate many of the tools common to Lean Sigma, Six Sigma, and other methodologies such as TQM. TQM is a term coined by American management consultants, including W. Edwards Deming, Joseph Juran, and Phil Crosby who published the classic book Quality Is Free in 1979.

However, continuous improvement is not just an American philosophy. *Kaizen* is the Japanese word for continuous improvement. It means a series of ongoing incremental improvements focused on eliminating all forms of waste from an operation. *Kaizen events* are improvement projects of short duration.

| Lean | Six Sigma | Project Management | Total Quality Management (TQM) |
|---|---|---|---|
| Continuous improvement methodology originally developed by Toyota to systematically identify and eliminate waste throughout a process or an organization. | Continuous improvement methodology originally developed by Motorola to reduce variation and is a registered service mark and trademark of Motorola, Inc. | Discipline of planning, organizing, and managing resources to bring about the successful completion of a specific project. | Inclusive philosophy that incorporates many of the tools common to Lean, Six Sigma, and Project Management for continuously improving the quality of products and processes. |

While both Lean and Six Sigma had their roots in manufacturing, as previously stated, Lean Six Sigma methodologies can be applied to almost any industry, including:

- Service organizations
- Healthcare
- Government
- Manufacturing
- Low-tech or high-tech operations
- Any organization with leadership committed to continuous improvement

## Lean Six Sigma Projects and the Project Management Life Cycle

Lean Six Sigma projects follow a typical project management life cycle. The difference in these projects is that the tools commonly associated with Lean, Six Sigma, and Total Quality Management are incorporated.

The chart below and descriptions that follow illustrate the tools commonly associated with Lean, Six Sigma, and Total Quality Management. However, it is not meant to be complete in all details. It allows for customization to fit the needs of a specific project. Each project starts with an "Idea" and follows the typical project phases: Initiate, Plan, Execute, and Close.

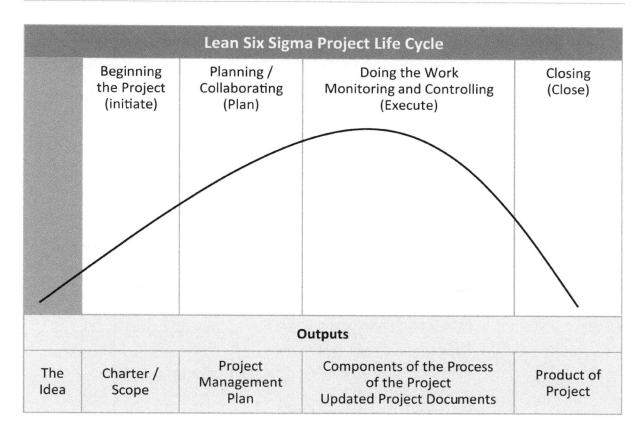

| Lean Six Sigma Project Life Cycle | | | |
|---|---|---|---|
| Beginning the Project (initiate) | Planning / Collaborating (Plan) | Doing the Work Monitoring and Controlling (Execute) | Closing (Close) |

**Outputs**

| The Idea | Charter / Scope | Project Management Plan | Components of the Process of the Project Updated Project Documents | Product of Project |
|---|---|---|---|---|

**TIME**

| Phase | Description/Purpose | Deliverables/Tools |
|---|---|---|
| **Idea** | • Preliminary and general description of a project idea and review of potential benefits. | • Identify problematic process<br>• Preliminary idea appraisal<br>• Decision: yes or no |
| **Initiate**: Define project requirements and scope | • Identify and document business needs and requirements<br>• Define project scope, goals, and objectives<br>• Identify project client, sponsor, and other stakeholders<br>• Develop initial estimates of effort, cost, schedule, and risk<br>• Identify deliverables and acceptance criteria | • A3 Current State (Left Side)<br>• Project Issue<br>• Background and Costs<br>  – Initial Gemba walk<br>  – Observation worksheet<br>  – Project scope statement/Charter<br>  – Team creation<br>  – SIPOC Diagram<br>  – Customer requirements and voice of customer communication |

1

| Phase | Description/Purpose | Deliverables/Tools |
|---|---|---|
| **Plan:** Plan project from beginning to end | • Define tasks, dependencies, and duration<br>• Refine resource requirements<br>• Develop work plan, milestones, and schedule<br>• Define the project control process, standards, and procedures<br>• Develop a risk management plan<br>• Identify communication needs<br>• Refine and manage expectations | • Current State Value Stream Map<br>• Situation Analysis<br>— Check sheets<br>— Spaghetti Diagram<br>— 5S<br>— Brainstorming<br>— Pareto Diagram and Analysis<br>— Cause and Effect Diagram<br>— 5Whys<br>— QFD<br>— Risk Analysis and Management Plan<br>• Goal and target |
| **Execute:** Do the work while monitoring and controlling the project | • Track actual progress to planned progress<br>• Assess and report status<br>• Coordinate activities and resources<br>• Implement corrective actions and update estimates and project schedule<br>• Manage and support individual and team activities<br>• Manage project priorities<br>• Manage and resolve problems and conflicts<br>• Manage changes to project scope<br>• Assess the quality of deliverables<br>• Communicate work assignments, progress, and issues<br>• Evaluate the performance of individuals and teams | • A3 Future State (Right Side)<br>• Future State Value Stream Map<br>• Countermeasures<br>— Risk Mitigation<br>• Implementation Plan<br>— What<br>— Who<br>— When<br>— Done?<br>• Cost/Benefit Analysis<br>— Return on Investment (ROI)<br>— Payback<br>• Checks<br>— Poka-Yoke (Mistake Proofing)<br>— Kanban (Visual Management)<br>— Total Productive Maintenance (TPM)<br>• Follow-Up Actions |

| Phase | Description/Purpose | Deliverables/Tools |
|---|---|---|
| **Close**: Close and report success level to sponsor and stakeholders | • Deliver project results<br>• Formally end the project<br>• Evaluate the performance of the project teams, team members, and the project manager<br>• Evaluate the project, draw conclusions, and document changes and lessons learned<br>• Identify areas of potential improvement for future projects | • Conclusion<br>– Project report and presentation<br>– Lessons learned<br>• Closing<br>– Formally end project |

1

## WHAT TO DO:

- ☑ Describe the differences and commonalities between the Lean and Six Sigma methodologies.

- ☑ Think about products you rely on in your daily life and how they have changed over the past decade.

- ☐ Identify one product or service that is a source of frustration for you and that needs improvement.

Other actions:

- ☐ _____

- ☐ _____

- ☐ _____

{ Lean - reduces waste, main focus is what the customer needs
Six Sigma - streamlines business processes

• Phones - they constantly have more helpful features . Also, google home and bluetooth technology

**Remember**

✓ In today's global business environment, pursuing continuous improvement is not a fad: It is a necessity.

✓ While terms such as Total Quality Management, Lean, and Six Sigma may take on specific meanings within organizations, the underlying tools and techniques may be widely applied.

✓ Understanding specific tools and how to apply them is a valuable workplace skill.

1

**Enhance Your Learning**

Watch the seven-minute review of Concept 1: What is Lean-Sigma?

***Concept 1: What is Lean-Sigma?*** (2016) (click on the image to launch video)

For definitions of Lean and Six Sigma, and related terms, visit the following websites:

***Lean Six Sigma Glossary*** (2020)

***Lean Sigma Toolbox*** (2020)

Watch the four-minute video about the history of Lean thinking and improvement strategies by David Hunter:

**The History of Lean Thinking** (2013)

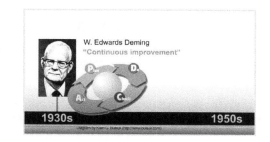

Watch the following two-minute video by the Netherlands Lean Six Sigma Company to see the power of combining the two methods:

**What is Lean Six Sigma? The power of combining the two methods** (2014)

Watch this six-minute video by the Virtual Kaizen Coach that describes the difference between Lean and Six Sigma:

**What is the Difference Between Lean and Six Sigma** (2020)

**Frustrating Product or Service**. Take a moment to consider what the business world was like five or ten years ago. Reflect on the products offered, customer expectations, quality levels, and delivery times. It is likely that customers today and, in the future, will expect a more extensive assortment of products and services, higher quality, better reliability, lower prices, and immediate delivery.

What products or services do you rely on in your daily life? Are any products or services a source of frustration to you? For example, have you experienced poor quality, long wait time, or a too costly product?

From a customer standpoint, identify one product or service that is a source of frustration to you. Explain why and describe whether it is a people or process issue that needs improvement.

Product or service: Oil changes/car maintenance    My cellphone

Why is it frustrating?

Oil changes/car maintenance → making appointments, dropping off my car and being without a car, and then picking up again

cellphone - my previous phone had the fingerprint screen on the back where my index finger naturally went but the new one has it on the front of the screen

Describe whether it is a people or a process issue that needs improvement.

Oil changes → service issue. It would be nice if someone just came to the house or if your car was picked up and dropped off.

Positive service - airport concierge where they get in your car, take you to the airport, park your car, then bring it to you when your flight returns.

Cellphone - design issue

# Describe Lean and Categories of Waste

2

Lean was developed by Toyota and is based on eliminating waste or Muda as it is called in Japan. Lean is typically a bottoms-up methodology. That means the decision to pursue various initiatives comes from the bottom of the organization or the people of a business unit doing the actual work. In addition to Muda, many other Japanese terms are commonly used in Lean. Some of them are as follows:

- Mura – describes unevenness in a process
- Muri – refers to overburdening or relying too much on one part of a process
- Kaizen – means continuous improvement
- Kanban – is a visual system that typically uses cards or stickers to control and alert people when inventories or flow problems occur
- Poka-Yoke – means to mistake-proof a process

This Concept covers essential principles and tools for a better understanding of categories of waste. You will learn how to describe wasteful practices in a work setting as viewed by customers.

## Voice of the Customer

As legendary leadership guru Peter Drucker stated years ago, "Quality in a product or service is not what the supplier puts in. It is what the customer gets out and is willing to pay for. A product is not quality because it is hard to make and costs a lot of money, as manufacturers typically believe. This is incompetence. Customers pay only for what gives them value. Nothing else constitutes quality."

Reflect on Drucker's comments as they relate to your experience with customers, and to what constitutes quality and waste in these typical work processes:

- Registering for a conference or event
- Checking into a hotel
- Making reservations at a restaurant
- Getting reimbursed for travel
- Preparing a business proposal
- Making a bank cash withdrawal
- Obtaining supplies or equipment
- Photocopying documents

Consider who the employees of many large organizations are trying to satisfy. Is it the customer or their boss? Think about how most large organizations are organized and what their organizational charts look like, and the messages the charts convey.

What would happen if we turned the traditional organizational structure upside down?

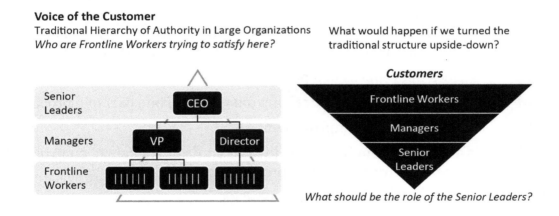

**Voice of the Customer**
Traditional Hierarchy of Authority in Large Organizations
*Who are Frontline Workers trying to satisfy here?*

What would happen if we turned the traditional structure upside-down?

*What should be the role of the Senior Leaders?*

What should leaders and employees try to do? The answer: satisfy customer needs. With the upside-down organizational chart, and with leadership support, employees would be more motivated to address process issues to better meet customer needs.

Quality Function Deployment (QFD), or Voice of the Customer (VOC), is a method intended to transform *user demands* into *design quality*, to deploy the functions forming quality, and to deploy methods for achieving the design quality into subsystems and component parts, and ultimately to specific elements. QFD was initially described by Dr. Yoji Akao, who developed QFD in Japan in the 1960s. It is illustrated by his House of Quality, which is illustrated in the simplified example below.

QFD helps planners focus on the characteristics of a new or existing product or service from the viewpoint of the customer. VOC methods consider customer needs, demands, expectations, preferences, and aversions.

QFD also considers the relationship between customer needs and product or service characteristics by transforming customer needs and technical requirements into the characteristics of the product or service. It prioritizes each product or service characteristic while simultaneously assessing the technical characteristics and setting development or satisfaction targets.

## Voice of the Customer and the House of Quality

Adapted from works of Dr. Yoji Akao

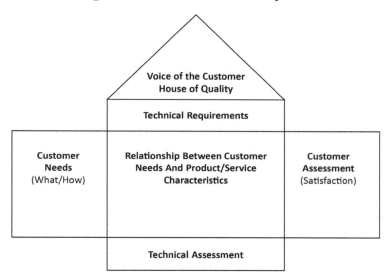

## Voice of the Customer and Lean as a Continuous Improvement Methodology

The goals of continuous improvement are to focus on the voice of the customer and to change processes and policies to eliminate waste and problems. In other words, the goals are to do it right the first time and every time and to meet or exceed customer expectations.

By definition, the traditional focus of Lean is to systematically identify and eliminate waste throughout an organization. Toyota's Total Production System (TPS), a methodology developed at Toyota under the guidance of Taiichi Ohno, is synonymous with Lean production. The philosophy of TPS is that all process activities can be divided into either adding value or creating waste (Muda). The goal of TPS is to maximize value by eliminating waste and it is applicable to any process.

## Categories of Waste

*Muda* is a Japanese term that expresses waste, uselessness, or futility in time. It can apply to a process or to resources. Following are common types of waste found in many organizations. They can also be translated into a waste of money:

### Underutilized Intellect and Skill Abuse

- Untapped skills – not asking people who do the job for input
- Underutilizing employee skills and abilities
- Using antiquated business tools and systems
- Limited employee empowerment
- Control and command leadership styles

### Waiting

- Approvals from others – next operation waiting
- Information from others
- Equipment or system repairs or maintenance
- Equipment or systems downtime and unplanned interruptions that occur due to inefficiencies
- Delays due to the scheduling of people or resources

### Excess Motion

- Walking to or from equipment or work areas
- Hunting or searching for proper supplies or materials
- Traveling to other offices or buildings
- Manual operations that could be automated
- Too many people involved

### Extra processing

- Extra samples, reports, copies
- Unnecessary information or operations
- Excessive cost accounting or reporting
- Multiple re-entries of data
- Excessive approval paths

### Over Processing

- Purchasing more than needed
- Making more product than ordered
- Making product components before an order is received
- Making product before people are ready for it
- Working unnecessary overtime

**Unnecessary Inventory**

- Excess material and supplies
- Unnecessary literature and reports
- Obsolete equipment
- Excess preprinted labels and forms
- Unnecessary files

**Transportation**

- Excess movement of goods or work-in-process
- Multiple approvals and hand-offs of paperwork
- Excessive emails or numerous people copied
- Unnecessary travel
- Misdirected calls

**Corrections, Rework, and Scrap**

- Any product or service that does not meet specifications and therefore either needs to be reworked or scrapped
- Product or service defects
- Design errors
- Change orders
- Staff and leadership turnover
- Lost customers

Think about all these common types of waste. Then consider the wisdom of Joseph Juran who established the 85/15 Rule. It states that at least 85 percent of problems (or wasteful attributes) are in systems.

> **The 85/15 Rule**
>
> *"At least 85% of problems are in the system — fewer than 15% are attributable to some particular individual or set of circumstances."*
>
> - Joseph Juran, Ph. D., 1955

## Theory of Constraints

Another critical philosophy related to the concept of continuous improvement is the Theory of Constraints (TOC). Eliyahu Goldratt introduced it in his classic 1980s book *The Goal*. This continuous improvement philosophy stresses the importance of identifying the weak links in a process with an understanding that a chain is no stronger than its weakest link.

Finding and eliminating system problems, the weakest links in a process and the most significant contributors to waste, are the challenges and focus of the Lean methodology.

---

### Process Improvement Case Study: More Problematic Than Thought!

**Current State**: A hospital's remote in-house pharmacy was costing more than it should and was identified as an area to examine for improvement. Prescription orders were written for patients and routinely sent to the hospital's pharmacy for processing. Depending on the time of day received, some prescriptions might be filed early in the day and sit there most of the day awaiting pick-up and delivery. This was not a major issue except for prescriptions requiring refrigeration where there was a threat of spoilage.

**Future State**: Using Lean tools the pharmacy improvement team started by brainstorming problematic work areas and areas of concern, categories of waste, and ideas for improvement. The team initially focused on the pharmacy's remote location and proposed relocating it to a central location. However, they quickly realized that a much bigger problem existed with the refrigerated drugs. They then also focused on streamlining the floorplan layout and reworking their standard practices to ensure that prescriptions would be properly handled, stored, and dispensed.

**Impact**: Streamlining pharmacy operations reduced cost and eliminated a potentially deadly situation.

---

### WHAT TO DO:

☐ Be mindful that customers pay only for what is of use to them and gives them value.

☐ Recognize that at least 85 percent of problems (and waste) are in systems.

☐ Identify one work process you believe warrants further examination for improvement

Other actions:

☐ _____

☐ _____

☐ _____

2

✓ "Quality in a product or service is not what the supplier puts in. It is what the customer gets out and is willing to pay for. A product is not quality because it is hard to make and costs a lot of money, as manufacturers typically believe. This is incompetence. Customers pay only for what is of use to them and gives them value. Nothing else constitutes quality." – Peter F. Drucker

✓ "The most dangerous kind of waste is the waste we do not recognize." – Shigeo Shingo

✓ If you do not look for waste, you may not see it.

✓ A productive place to start is by identifying processes that are either problematic or frustrating to you or others in your organization.

✓ "At least 85% of problems are in systems – fewer than 15% are attributable to some particular individual or set of circumstances" – Joseph Juran

✓ A chain is only as strong as its weakest link

Watch the six-minute review of Concept 2 – Part 1 and 2:

***Lean and Categories of Waste*** (2016)
Part 1

(click on the image to launch video)

KEY CONCEPT 2 – PART I
LEAN AND CATEGORIES OF WASTE

**Enhance Your Learning**

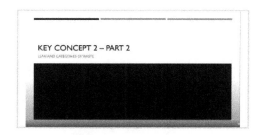

***Lean and Categories of Waste*** (2016)
Part 2

Learn more about Quality Function Deployment by watching the following three-minute video. QFD is a rigorous method for translating customer needs, wants, and wishes into step-by-step procedures for delivering a product or service. While delivering better designs tailored to customer needs, QFD may also cut the normal development cycle significantly. QFD uses the QFD House of Quality (a template in the QI Macros) to help structure your thinking, which will help ensure nothing is left out. Watch ***QFD House of Quality Template in Excel*** by QI Macros (2010):

***Quality Function Deployment (QFD) Example*** (2019)

Read about examples of business process improvement in The House of Quality (2016) by Harvard Business Review:

***The House of Quality*** (2016)

Review the slide-deck "House of Quality" developed by Muhammad Haris. It illustrates QFD by discussing pizza.

***QFD for Pizza*** (2016)

Watch the following fifteen-minute video about Quality Function Deployment (QFD) and House of Quality:

***Quality Function Deployment (QFD) House of Quality*** (2019)

2

**Problematic Work Process**. Previously, you identified from a customer standpoint one product or service that is either problematic or frustrating to you. Now consider common work processes in your organization (or one you are familiar with) that may be problematic or frustrating to internal or external customers. For example, you might identify a process like one of these:

- Getting to work on time
- Registering for a conference or event
- Planning a celebratory event for a co-worker
- Completing a travel expense report
- Improving an organization's approval process
- Renewing insurance coverage
- Paying invoices
- Preparing financial statements
- Preparing a business proposal
- Preparing for a client visit
- Making a business presentation
- Making a bank cash deposit or withdrawal
- Obtaining supplies or equipment
- Preparing a production schedule
- Photocopying documents
- Processing a customer order
- Conducting a test or audit
- Improving a facilities layout
- Moving an office or workspace

- Recruiting for a job position
- Preparing for a job interview
- Selecting a job candidate

Once you identify a problematic or frustrating work process, review the common types of waste (Muda). Reflect on the wisdom of Joseph Juran that 85 percent of problems (or wastes) are in the system. Respond to the following while considering that this process may also serve as an area of focus for applying the continuous improvement tools described later in this guide.

Problematic Work Process: _____

Process Description: _____

_____

_____

_____

_____

_____

_____

_____

_____

_____

_____

_____

_____

_____

_____

_____

_____

_____

2

Why Selected (problem or frustration):

*It's our job every day to make every important aspect of the customer experience a little bit better.*

– Jeff Bezos

# Observe Processes and Scope Improvement Initiatives

This Concept covers essential principles and tools for better understanding how to observe processes and scope improvement initiatives. You will learn about the importance of first observing work processes and understanding the situation before you attempt to make improvements.

Observation of process value streams (or lack thereof, in other words, waste) and questioning the status quo of a process are the initial steps for any continuous process improvement initiative.

The term *value stream* describes the necessary factors that contribute to the value of a product or service from the viewpoint of the customer. *Waste* is something that does not add value to the customer and that is not needed by any part of the process. In engineering and project management, nice-to-haves and extras added to a project (often referred to as gold plating) but not specified in the contract scope of work are considered to be waste if the customer is not willing to pay for them.

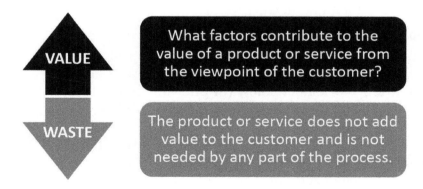

**Gemba walk**. *Gemba* is a Japanese term that translates to "the real place," meaning, in the context of processes improvement, the place where the work is completed, and the value of the product or service created. *Gemba walk* refers to observing a process to assess the situation and gain firsthand knowledge of what is occurring. The frequency and duration of a gemba walk depends on the needs of the organization.

Individuals who participate in a Gemba walk make in-person observations at the site where the work is done. Observers may do this as part of a team or individually. The objective is to observe a process rather than to find fault or enforce organization policies. Interaction with employees in a nonjudgmental manner can be an effective method to obtain details about a process that cannot be learned solely by observation.

Observing a process is a powerful, yet simple tool; variations, and their causes, are major enemies. However, you must plan the observation procedure before you begin. Consider this: How do you define a process and from where do you observe it? For example, do you observe it from 30,000 feet, one foot, or one inch? The answer: It depends!

During the Gemba walk, observers typically make notes of the steps or activities in the process, their timing, and any issues or concerns. However, observers do not try to solve or improve the process during the observation.

Following the observation, the observers may ask workers for their ideas for process improvement. Then, the observers take time to reflect and gather additional information and data if needed to identify the scope of potential improvement activities.

Some of the questions to answer in the Gemba walk or observation process are as follows:

- Where does the process begin and end?
- What steps are included in the process?
- How could you observe and track waste?
- What would you measure?

Use the Observation Worksheet below (or one you create) to observe someone making toast. An Observation Worksheet is also available in Appendix B.

Sketch the layout of the toast-making work area in the upper right corner of the worksheet. Document the activities the person performs as they make toast and track the time to complete each activity. Then indicate areas of waste by placing an X in the appropriate boxes. Finally, note any issues.

OBSERVATION WORKSHEET

Process: _____
Person Observed: _____
Location: _____
Observer: _____
Date: _____
Start Time: _____  Finish: _____

Layout of Work Area

**Sketch Layout of Work Area**

## Sample Process Observation Worksheet

**Categories of Waste**

| Times | Activity | OPERATION | WAITING | EXCESS MOTION | EXTRA PROCESSING | OVER PRODUCING | UNNECESSARY INVENTORY | TRANSPORTATION | CORRECTIONS, REWORK & SCRAP | UNDERUTILIZED PEOPLE | Notes |
|---|---|---|---|---|---|---|---|---|---|---|---|
| : : | | | | | | | | | | | |
| : : | | | | | | | | | | | |
| : : | | | | | | | | | | | |
| : : | | | | | | | | | | | |
| : : | | | | | | | | | | | |
| : : | | | | | | | | | | | |
| : : | | | | | | | | | | | |
| : : | | | | | | | | | | | |
| : : | | | | | | | | | | | |
| : : | | | | | | | | | | | |
| : : | | | | | | | | | | | |
| : : | | | | | | | | | | | |

**Process Steps or Activities with Times**

As indicated, one of the first questions to answer in observing any process is: Where does the process begin and end? A problem people often experience the first time they try applying a continuous improvement methodology (particularly Lean Sigma or Six Sigma) is they try to solve "world hunger." In other words, they do not narrow the scope of their process review to something reasonable and doable, something they can observe and chart.

 **Spaghetti Diagram**. Another useful tool in the observation process is a Spaghetti diagram, which is a visual representation of what **occurs** during a process. A Spaghetti diagram, which is also called a String diagram, illustrates the movement (travel) of people, materials, equipment, or information **in a defined work area**. It is helpful for analyzing the current state of a process as well as for planning its future state.

To make a spaghetti diagram, draw a continuous line (preferably in pencil) from point to point to depict the movement from start to finish. The continuous line illustrates redundancies and wastes in the process operation. These might be things such as:

- Waiting
- Excess motion
- Extra processing
- Overproduction

- Unnecessary inventory
- Excess transportation
- Rework and scrap
- Underutilized people or resources

While computer programs could be used to create a Spaghetti diagram, the most effective ones are made by people using pencil and paper and who observe actual movements at the work site.

As before, use the Observation Worksheet (or one you create) to document the process of someone making toast. But this time, after you sketch the layout of the person's work area, track the movement of the person in the work area.

Following is an example work area sketch and Spaghetti diagram:

**Current Condition: Making Toast in a Kitchen**

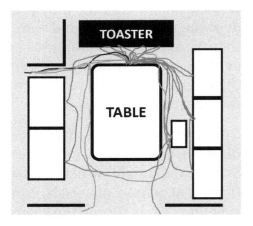

- The more spaghetti-like the diagram, the clearer the need for redesigned work!

- It is easy to see wasted time/travel when the diagram is complete.

- To better appreciate the waste, you can add distance and time measurements, and calculate the unnecessary distance traveled and wasted time.

After you observe your target process and understand its complexities, document the objectives for a possible process improvement project by completing a Lean Project Scope Statement. This will assist you in defining and communicating the scope of process improvement ideas, and in gauging the leadership support needed for improvement actions.

Following is a sample Lean Project Scope Statement. A Lean Project Scope Statement worksheet is also available in Appendix A.

In project management, a scope statement may serve as a Project Charter with the initial elements outlined and then later refined.

## Lean Six Sigma Project Scope Statement

Work Process: _____

Participants: _____

_____

Process description:

_____

_____

_____

_____

_____

_____

_____

_____

_____

_____

_____

Why Selected:

_____

_____

_____

_____

3

Objectives:

_____

_____

_____

_____

Sponsor:

_____

## The Four Rules of Lean

By definition, a process typically involves steps and decisions in the way work is accomplished, and usually follows a sequence of events. There are **four basic rules** associated with applying Toyota's Total Production System (TPS) or **Lean methodology** approach to process improvement:

1.  All work is specified as to content, sequence, timing, and outcome.

2.  Every customer-supplier connection must be direct, and there must be an unambiguous yes-or-no way to send requests and receive responses.

3.  The pathway for every product and service must be simple and direct.

4.  Any improvement must be made by using the scientific method, under the guidance of an instructor, and at the lowest possible level in the organization.

The *scientific method* refers to a body of techniques for investigating phenomena, acquiring new knowledge, and correcting and integrating previous knowledge. To be termed scientific, a method of inquiry must be based on gathering *observable and measurable* evidence. The scientific method consists of the collection of data through observation, experimentation, and the formulation and testing of hypotheses.

Observing processes and scoping improvement initiatives can serve as a preliminary Go/No-Go decision point in Lean methodology.

Keep the four rules and the scientific method in mind as we move to the next Concepts, which focus on diagramming processes by using flowcharts and process maps and collecting data on value streams.

## Process Improvement Case Study: Observe Processes and Stimulate Engagement

**Current State**: Working from home in the financial services industry, like other industries, has become commonplace. Representatives are still employed and continue to process business as usual with limited disruption to the customer experience. However, in some organizations the process of moving representatives from an office environment to working from home happened rapidly. The processes that had to be reviewed, confirmed effective, and put in place required input from those doing the jobs with direct observation of what worked and what did not. The goal was to keep workflow moving and staff engaged while working remotely.

**Future State**: Taking a team approach, ideas were brainstormed and studied to promote cross-training and segmenting of responsibilities during time crunch situations. Individual work processes were observed, and the scope of initiatives defined. Additional accountability through spot checks, PC monitoring worksheets, reviews and debriefs with managers, and iterative streamlining of the individual processes resulted in improve efficiency and effectiveness.

**Impact**: Empowering staff to observe, identify, and eliminate redundant and unnecessary approval paths helped streamline operations. This resulted in the organization being able to maintain employment levels while adding checks and balances to ensure that workflow progressed smoothly. Customers are happy and representatives are employed.

3

## WHAT TO DO:

☐ Observe a problematic work process and document your findings using an Observation Worksheet.

☐ Decide who should participate in possible improvement efforts.

☐ Complete a Lean Six Sigma Project Scope Statement for your work process.

Other actions:

☐

☐

☐

**Remember**

✓ "It has been my observation that most people get ahead during the time that others waste." – Henry Ford

✓ A process typically involves steps and decisions in the way work is accomplished, and usually follows a sequence of events.

✓ Narrow the scope of your process review and improvement initiative to something reasonable and doable.

✓ Follow a method of inquiry based on gathering *observable and measurable* evidence.

**Enhance Your Learning**

Watch the five-minute review of Concept 3:

***Observing Processes and Scoping Potential Improvement Initiatives*** (2016)

(click on the image to launch video)

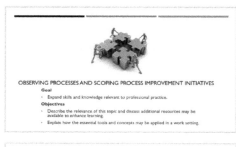

Watch the seven-minute video on Gemba walking.

***Gemba Walk: Where the Real Work Happens*** (2019)

Watch this five-minute to learn more about how to create a Spaghetti Diagram or Chart.

*Spaghetti Diagram* (2017)

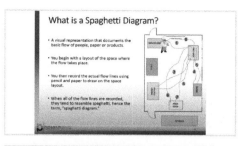

Watch the following five-minute video by GBMP on "Lean Thinking: Toast Kaizen," which overviews Lean with a focus on the process of making toast.

*Toast Kaizen – Introduction to Lean* (2008)

Watch this nine-minute TedTalk by Tom Wujec who introduces the design exercise to develop system thinking. It also discusses the importance of negotiating, teamwork and cooperation, conceptual thinking skills, and understanding systems. He makes an analogy of creating a system by showing the way people around the world make toast.

3

*Got a wicked problem? First, tell me how you make toast* (2013)

**Observe a Work Process**. Observe a problematic work process and document your findings using the Observation Worksheet that follows or make a worksheet of your own. Then complete a Lean Six Sigma Project Scope Statement. Blank worksheets are available in Appendix A and B.

## OBSERVATION WORKSHEET

| Process: _____ | Layout of Work Area |
|---|---|
| Person Observed: _____ | |
| Location: _____ | |
| Observer: _____ | |
| Date: _____ | |
| Start Time: _____ Finish: _____ | |

| Times | Activity | UUNDERUTILIZED INTELLECT | WAITING | EXCESS MOTION | EXTRA PROCESSING | OVER PRODUCING | UNNECESSARY INVENTORY | TRANSPORTATION | CORRECTIONS, REWORK & SCRAP | OTHER: | Notes |
|---|---|---|---|---|---|---|---|---|---|---|---|
| : : | | | | | | | | | | | |
| : : | | | | | | | | | | | |
| : : | | | | | | | | | | | |
| : : | | | | | | | | | | | |
| : : | | | | | | | | | | | |
| : : | | | | | | | | | | | |
| : : | | | | | | | | | | | |
| : : | | | | | | | | | | | |
| : : | | | | | | | | | | | |
| : : | | | | | | | | | | | |
| : : | | | | | | | | | | | |
| : : | | | | | | | | | | | |
| : : | | | | | | | | | | | |
| : : | | | | | | | | | | | |
| : : | | | | | | | | | | | |
| : : | | | | | | | | | | | |
| : : | | | | | | | | | | | |
| : : | | | | | | | | | | | |
| : : | | | | | | | | | | | |
| : : | | | | | | | | | | | |
| : : | | | | | | | | | | | |
| : : | | | | | | | | | | | |

## Lean Six Sigma Project Scope Statement

Work Process: _____

Participants: _____

_____

Process description:

_____

_____

_____

_____

Why Selected:

_____

_____

_____

_____

Objectives:

_____

_____

_____

_____

Sponsor:

_____

3

*There is nothing so useless as doing efficiently that which should not be done at all.*

– Peter Drucker

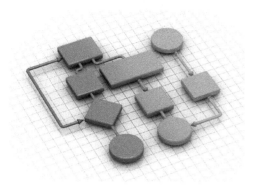

# Diagram Processes Using Flowcharts and Process Maps

This Concept covers essential principles and tools that describe how to diagram processes using flowcharts and process maps. It includes a description of a SIPOC diagram, which is a process map typically used to obtain a high-level view of a process before doing more in-depth analysis.

## What are Flowcharts and Process Maps?

**Flowcharts** and **process maps** are diagramming tools that you can use to illustrate processes. Diagrams make it easier for everyone to understand a process under review and to plan for analysis and improvements.

The terms flowchart and process map are often used interchangeably and refer to creating a diagram that illustrates a business process. The only difference between these words is that process mapping refers to the actual process of creating a diagram; the diagram itself is typically called a flowchart.

The steps or activities in a process are shown in various boxes, and their order is illustrated by arrows that connect the flow of process activities. Depending on the level of detail needed, in addition to boxes and arrows, flowcharts and process maps can also use other symbols, for example, circles, diamonds, ovals, or other shapes.

In the Lean sigma methodology, process steps are typically mapped from left to right. They detail the specific actions that are taken throughout the process or in a particular part of a process.

A high-level process map typically has five to seven overarching process steps; a detailed process map usually contains many more. One way to start developing a process map is to use a sticky note for the various process steps and place them in a line from left to right.

Following is an example of a high-level flowchart or process map for a generic process.

**Process Step #1** → **Process Step #2** → **Process Step #3**

Consider the simple high-level process of making toast. How many steps are there: 3, 7, 15? The answer is: It depends. You could consolidate various activities into larger process steps as long as you adhere to the four basic rules of the Lean methodology described in the previous Concept. As a reminder, here are the rules:

1. All work is specified as to content, sequence, timing, and outcome.

2. Every customer-supplier connection must be direct, and there must be an unambiguous yes-or-no way to send requests and receive responses.

3. The pathway for every product and service must be simple and direct.

4. Any improvement must be made by using the scientific method, under the guidance of an instructor, and at the lowest possible level in the organization.

### Making Toast: High-Level Flowchart

Obviously, your process for making toast may differ, but the diagram illustrates the general process of making toast.

As you begin to map a process, you may need to consider some issues that are not immediately apparent. Following are some ideas for how to identify and develop related concerns:

- Reflect on the customer and their expectations, and the steps in the process that add value for the customer and those that may be problematic.

- Review each process step and consider the financial impact and whether the business needs to improve the process.

- Consider the supply or value chain important to successfully completing each process step.

# What is a SIPOC diagram?

A **SIPOC** (**S**uppliers, **I**nputs, **P**rocess, **O**utputs, **C**ustomers) diagram is a high-level process map that describes a process as well as the boundaries of the project. You can use this tool to identify relevant components or vital elements of a process improvement initiative. The purpose of a SIPOC diagram is to illustrate process components and stakeholders, and thus to better understand and communicate the scope and complexity of an improvement initiative.

As a starting point for developing a SIPOC, identify the primary high-level process steps, and then identify the input, output, supplier, and customer components. The following diagram illustrates the typical format of a SIPOC worksheet.

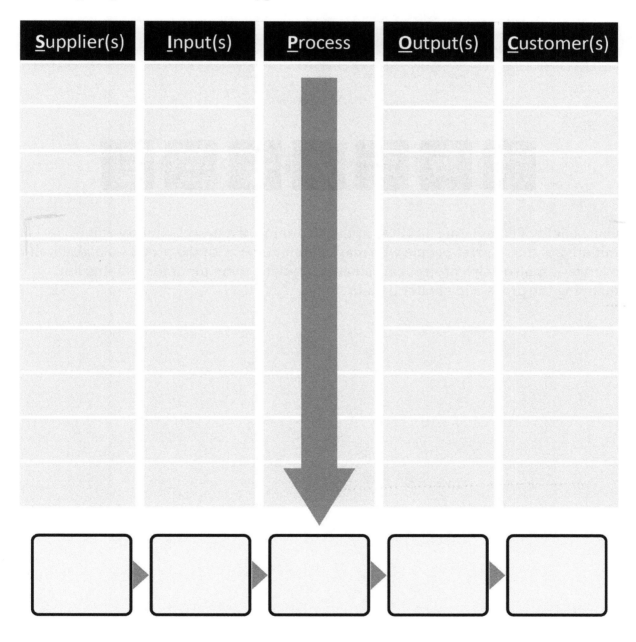

Following is an example of a completed SIPOC diagram that illustrates the process of making toast.

## Completed SIPOC Diagram: Making Toast

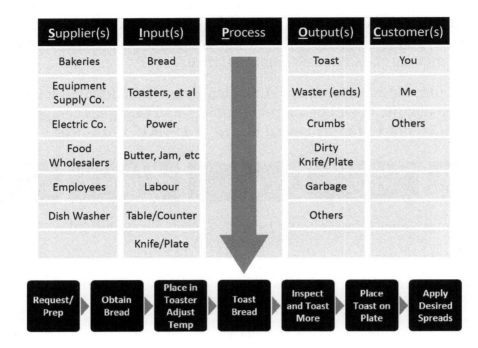

| **S**upplier(s) | **I**nput(s) | **P**rocess | **O**utput(s) | **C**ustomer(s) |
|---|---|---|---|---|
| Bakeries | Bread | | Toast | You |
| Equipment Supply Co. | Toasters, et al | | Waster (ends) | Me |
| Electric Co. | Power | | Crumbs | Others |
| Food Wholesalers | Butter, Jam, etc | | Dirty Knife/Plate | |
| Employees | Labour | | Garbage | |
| Dish Washer | Table/Counter | | Others | |
| | Knife/Plate | | | |

Request/ Prep → Obtain Bread → Place in Toaster Adjust Temp → Toast Bread → Inspect and Toast More → Place Toast on Plate → Apply Desired Spreads

**4**

One benefit of completing a SIPOC at the beginning of a process improvement initiative is that it gives people who may be unfamiliar with the process a high-level overview. It also helps project participants by giving them input for defining and mapping the process in greater detail.

## Process Improvement Case Study: Make Copies at Your Own Risk

**Current State**: Consider developing a simple flowchart for a process like making copies of a report. The steps and process activities might include gathering documents to copy, walking from desk to copier, making the copies, walking from copier to desk, distributing the copies, and filing personal copy.

A flowchart like the following makes it easy to see the process at a glance:

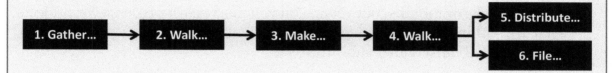

However, we all know and have experienced what can happen to a simple process like this with paper jams, toner issues, unexpected copier conversations, and the like. Such interruptions can be frustrating; however, they also significantly escalate the cost.

**Future State**: If you consider the total cost, outsourcing the process to a copy shop may be a better alternative, especially for larger projects.

**Impact**: Reduce stress, waste, and cost.

### WHAT TO DO:

- ☐ Observe a problematic work process and document your findings using an Observation Worksheet.
- ☐ Decide who should participate in possible improvement efforts.
- ☐ Complete a Lean Six Sigma Project Scope Statement for your work process.

Other actions:

☐ _____

☐ _____

☐ _____

**Remember**

✓ Process improvement initiatives within organizations can sometimes seem to be overwhelming and may involve political and bureaucratic complexities. Keeping your focus on Toyota's proven lean philosophy and methodology will help you keep things simple.

✓ You must focus on initiatives that are doable within a reasonable time, such as several weeks or months, not years; and you must select processes or projects that are within your or your team's span of control. Many large processes can be segmented into smaller sub-processes.

✓ Start with improving the lower order processes that will have the most significant impact on your organization.

**Enhance Your Learning**

4

Watch the four-minute review of Concept 4:

***Flow Charting and Process Mapping*** (2016)

(click on the image to launch video)

Watch a four-minute overview of process flow charts by Cody Baldwin.

***Introduction to Process Flow Charts (Lean Six Sigma)*** (2020)

This three-minute video explains the four principles of Total Productive Maintenance (TPM) and its impact on an organization to reduce downtime, increase quality, and improve performance.

***Four Principles TPM by Four Principles*** (2013)

Watch how to create a SIPOC. This nine-minute video illustrates a simple way to develop a professional looking SIPOC.

***SIPOC Diagram Simplified [SIPOC Tutorial]*** (2019)

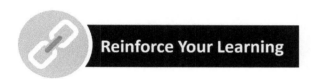

**SIPOC Diagram**. For the work process you identified as the focus for applying Lean tools and methodologies, develop a SIPOC diagram using the sample worksheet below or apply the tips from the Enhance Your Learning video and develop a SIPOC using Excel. A SIPOC Worksheet is available in Appendix C.

4

| SIPOC for: | Team members:_____ | Date: |
|------------|------------------------------------------|-------|
| _____ | _____ | _____ |

| **S**upplier(s) | **I**nput(s) | **P**rocess | **O**utput(s) | **C**ustomer(s) |
|-----------------|--------------|-------------|---------------|-----------------|
|                 |              |             |               |                 |
|                 |              |             |               |                 |
|                 |              |             |               |                 |
|                 |              |             |               |                 |
|                 |              |             |               |                 |
|                 |              |             |               |                 |
|                 |              |             |               |                 |
|                 |              |             |               |                 |
|                 |              |             |               |                 |
|                 |              |             |               |                 |

4

# Collect Data on Value Streams

## What is a Value Stream Map (VSM)?

A VSM is a sophisticated flowchart that typically includes a visual picture of a process incorporating symbols, essential metrics or measures such as time, number of defects, output, delays, dollars, and so on.

A VSM can be a view of a process from 10,000 feet, 1,000 feet, one foot, or from inches. From whatever view you select, the next step is to identify all major activities and determine if they are **value-adding** or **non-value adding**.

In general, a VSM has three main components. The first is documenting how the request to improve a process is communicated. This helps establish the scope of an improvement initiative. The second component, the process map or flowchart, has situational factors appropriately noted. The third component is the metrics relevant to the process.

### Takt Time

For many standardized processes, well-established process steps and metrics or performance standards may already exist, which creates a baseline for performance. **Takt time** is a calculation that compares the time available to do work by the customer demand for a product or service. *Takt time* is derived from the German word Taktzeit, which translates to the cycle time, pace, or rate at which process steps are completed.

In Lean, Takt time is the rate at which a finished product needs to be completed to meet customer demand. If an organization has a Takt time of five minutes, that means every five minutes a complete product, assembly, or item must be delivered from the operational process because, on average, a customer is procuring the finished product every five minutes. Stated mathematically, Takt time = available time for production / required units of production.

5

## Takt Time and Our Toast Example

Using our making toast example, assume a kitchen is available for 20 minutes in the morning. Customer demand is 5 slices of toast per day. Then the Takt time is: 20 minutes / 5 slices = 4 minutes. As a result, the kitchen must process one slice of output every four minutes.

For most processes, Takt time is intended to be an average measure of output. There are variations around the calculated number; however, on average the process should meet the number. A VSM is useful because it identifies current areas of inconsistency or problems with essential metrics. The VSM provides a picture or snapshot of the current or as-is state of the process, and it also serves as a basis or springboard for developing a future state map.

The illustration below is an example of a simple VSM incorporating a Saw-tooth diagram with process metrics. The solid black triangles indicate delays.

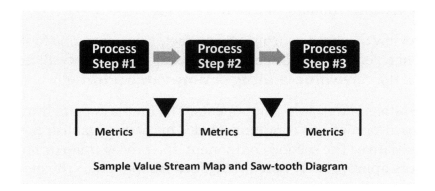

Sample Value Stream Map and Saw-tooth Diagram

Following are some common symbols used in VSMs.

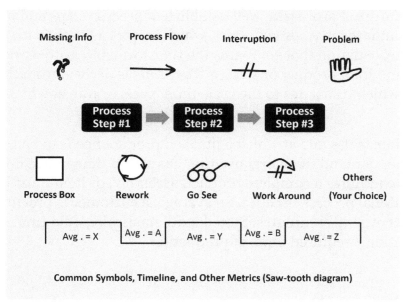

Common Symbols, Timeline, and Other Metrics (Saw-tooth diagram)

# Drawing Value Stream Maps

Simple is good! Using Lean Sigma methodologies, we suggest you draw Value Stream Maps in pencil on paper no larger than 11 x 17 inches to promote simplicity and ease of change.

Following is a sample Value Stream Map Worksheet that is often preprinted and bound in a tablet to be distributed to departments. The worksheet helps guide novices through the completion of a VSM and reminds them of the various symbols commonly used to illustrate communication methods and flow, people involved, process activities, and potential problems.

Common communication and transmission symbols are illustrated in the **upper part of the printed worksheet**.

## Value Stream Map (VSM) Worksheet

Following are commonly used communication and transmission symbols*:

**Communication Transmission Symbols**

| Computer | Written | Mail | Verbal | Customer |
|----------|---------|------|--------|----------|

**Process Step #1**

Transmit Requests or Order

Fax   Telephone

Start by inserting a symbol for the client or person making the initial request in the upper right-corner. Next, enter the other communication and transmission symbols (right to left) to reflect communication handoffs and illustrate the importance of clear and accurate communications and alternative transmission methods.

Then insert the flowchart or process map steps (left to right) in the middle part of the printed worksheet.

5

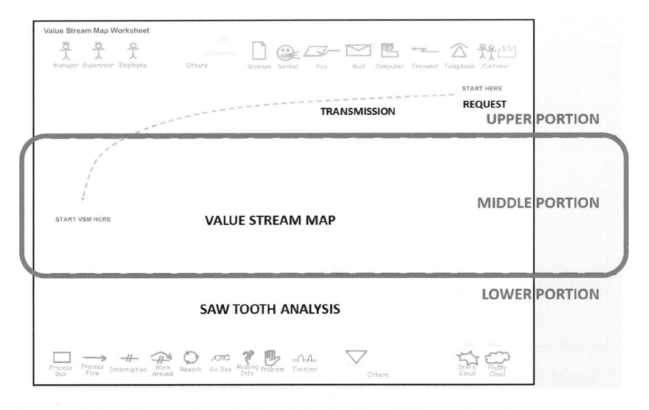

Selected symbols and icons are from the Noun Project by: Mourad Mokrane, Sergey Furtaev, and Richard Wearn. Other icons by Spencer Harrison, Ziggy, artworkbean, and Stock Image Folio.

Insert the metrics in the **bottom part of the printed worksheet**.

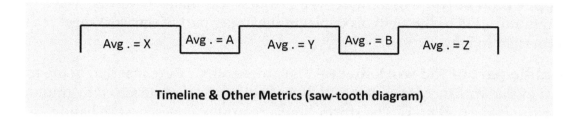

**Timeline & Other Metrics (saw-tooth diagram)**

Here is a quick reference for the steps to draw a VSM:

1.  Insert the name of the client or person making a request in the upper right corner of the VSM worksheet.

2.  Add all the ways requests or transmissions are made across the top (from right to left).

3.  Draw the VSM process steps across the center of the page starting at the left side.

4.  Add process steps (from left to right). Finish with the client or person having the request satisfied.

5.  Insert a Saw-tooth diagram across the bottom. Show the critical metrics, including delays and when nothing is happening.

5

## Example 1: Value Stream Map (VSM): Making Toast

**Upper part of the worksheet** – The request was made by verbal communication as the symbols depict in the upper part of the worksheet reading from right to left.

**Middle part of the worksheet** – The process steps were inserted in the middle part of the worksheet from left to right with other symbols inserted to graphically illustrate the conditions. The storm clouds represent concerns; the hand represents a problem; the circle with arrows indicates an area requiring rework; and the glasses and magnifying glass indicate areas needing a closer look.

**Lower part of the worksheet** – The metrics were inserted in the lower part of the worksheet as depicted by the Saw-tooth diagram. The upside-down triangles indicate dead time, though some people prefer to use tombstones.

The major **problem** area observed and causing excess delays was associated with **logistics**: locating and staging materials and utensils (bread, butter, jam, knife, plate, and so on.)

### Value Stream Map: Current State Making Toast

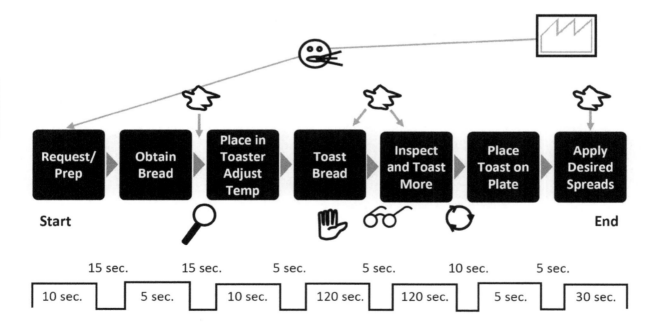

Overall: 5 min 55 sec.
Avg. Wait: 55 sec.
Avg. Process: 5 min

## Process Improvement Case Study: Select the Cheaper Hotel?

**Current State**: An optometrist decided to attend her annual convention being held in a major city. She researched hotels and decided to select a hotel $50 cheaper, but several miles from the convention site. This decision meant that she had to take an Uber to and from the site at the busiest times of the day, which caused her to miss some planned events. After returning home she decided to do a Lean analysis of her event planning process. The Value Stream Map that follows in "Example 2" depicts the process steps and metrics. As depicted, the Uber travel to and from the hotel added $50 to her costs. However, more importantly, over two hours were consumed in those travel steps.

**Future State**: The optometrist decided for future conventions that staying at a hotel within walking distance of the event would eliminate the unproductive travel time and commuting costs. The premium cost for selecting a hotel within walking distance is more than offset by the ability to maximize the educational value of the conference.

**Impact**: Reduction of unproductive travel time resulted in the optometrist being able to attend more convention functions, increase vendor networking time, lower overall costs, and reduce stress.

5

## Example 2: Value Stream Map (VSM): Select the Cheaper Hotel?

**Upper part of the worksheet** – The communication was first handled via computer followed by verbally communicating the request as the symbols depict in the upper part of the worksheet reading from right to left.

**Middle part of the worksheet** – The process steps were inserted in the middle part of the worksheet from left to right with multiple symbols inserted to graphically illustrate the conditions. The storm clouds placed over the travel steps indicate a major source of frustration for the traveler.

**Lower part of the worksheet** – The metrics were inserted in the lower part of the worksheet as depicted by the Saw-tooth diagram. The actual process time totaled 25 hours and 40 minutes and the wait or delay time total was 7 hours and 10 minutes. However, the most problematic area to focus on for future improvement for this traveler is the wasted time and frustration associated with getting to and from the hotel.

### Value Stream Map:

### Select the Cheaper Hotel?

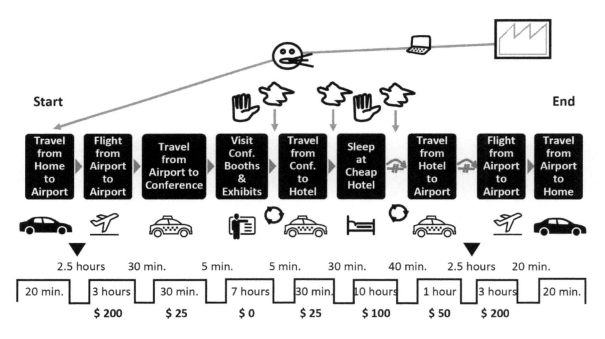

Overall Time: 32hr. 50min.
Wait Time: 7hr. 10min.
Process Time: 25hr. 40min.
Est. Cost: $ 600

## Process Improvement Case Study: Streamline Proposal Process

**Current State**: Two service organizations reviewed their client proposal processes to better understand delays in service. Both organizations received multiple requests for proposals, and this required staff to analyze the benefits and costs associated with the new projects in a short "window of opportunity."

A Value Stream Map (VSM) for each organization's proposal follows in "Example 3" and depicts the process steps and metrics. For Organization 1, the actual process time associated with the activities to develop the proposal was approximately 4.5 days. However, the wait time varied from 17 to 110 days. Organization 2 was even worse, with the actual process time being about 15 days, and the wait time between 56 and 325 days. The VSM clearly depicted the problem areas to be mostly in the consultation and peer collaboration process steps. A Cause and Effect Diagram was developed to separate and categorize the issues and to establish practical goals and targets, one of which was "Kill bad projects early."

**Future State**: A Future State VSM depicted an expedited preliminary Go/No Go review process to determine the merits of pursuing projects before time and effort was invested in a formal proposal analysis process. The goal of the expedited process is to vet concepts and reach consensus on whether to proceed (Go/NO GO Decision) within a one-week turnaround timeframe.

**Impact**: The bottom line is that considerable savings in time and money can be achieved by assembling and soliciting input from key stakeholders at the early proposal stage to determine Go/No go before investing in a detailed analysis.

5

## Example 3: Value Stream Map (VSM): Streamline Proposal Process

The following VSM illustrates the time (days in the Saw-tooth diagram) required by two actual organizations to respond to a client request for a new program proposal. The VSM maps the current process. The major **problem** in both organizations is **excessive wait / delay time**.

| Organization 1: | actual process time 4.5 days | |
|---|---|---|
| | wait / delay time 17 days (low) | + 4.5 = 21.5 days to respond |
| | wait / delay time 110 days (high) | + 4.5 = 114.5 days to respond |

| Organization 2: | actual process time 15 days | |
|---|---|---|
| | wait / delay time 56 days (low) | +15 = 71 days to respond |
| | wait / delay time 325 days (high) | +15= 330 days to respond |

### Value Stream Map: Streamline Proposal Process

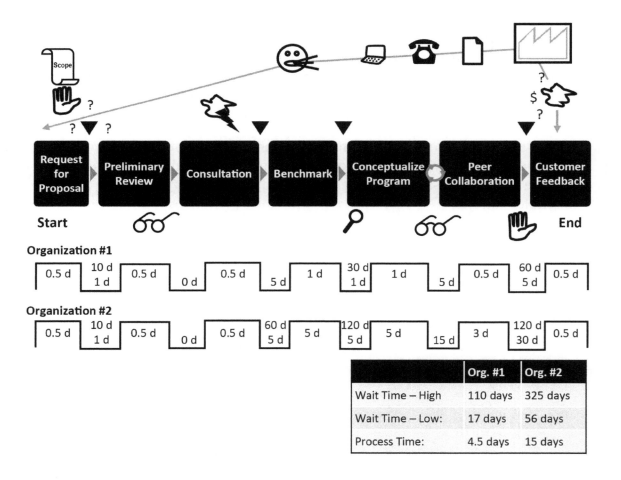

| | Org. #1 | Org. #2 |
|---|---|---|
| Wait Time – High | 110 days | 325 days |
| Wait Time – Low: | 17 days | 56 days |
| Process Time: | 4.5 days | 15 days |

## WHAT TO DO:

☐ Observe a problematic work process and document your findings using an Document how an improvement request will be communicated in the top part of the VSM worksheet.

☐ Insert your flowchart or process map with appropriate symbols in the middle part of the VSM worksheet.

☐ Insert the appropriate metrics using a Saw-tooth diagram in the lower part of the VSM worksheet.

Other actions:

☐ _____

☐ _____

☐ _____

✓ Lean methodology suggests you draw Value Stream Maps in pencil on 11" x 17" paper to promote simplicity and ease of change.

✓ Conventional symbols are often used to represent various actions or activities; however, you are free to use other symbols if they work better for you and your organization.

5

**Enhance Your Learning**

Watch the seven-minute review of Concept 5:

***Observing and Collecting Data on Value Streams*** (2016)

(click on the image to launch video)

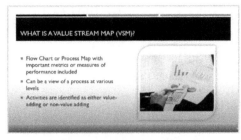

Watch the following 19-minute video about Value Stream Maps.

***How to Value Stream Map [STEP BY STEP]***

Watch the following two-minute video that explains how to draw Value Stream Maps by the Lean Sigma Academy.

***Lean Tools – Value Stream Mapping*** (2015)

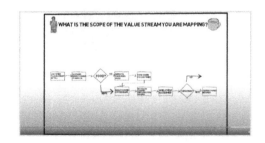

Watch the following thirteen-minute video explaining Takt time, cycle time, and lead time by OpsExcellence.

***Takt Time, Cycle Time, Lead Time*** (2015)

## Reinforce Your Learning

**Value Stream Map**. For the process you identified as the focus for applying Lean tools and methodologies, draw a Value Stream Map. Use the sample worksheet that follows, or the sample Value Stream Worksheet available in Appendix D, or create a template of your own.

Use the sample Observation Worksheet available in Appendix B to further document the process activities and metrics you will need to complete the Saw-toothed diagram in the bottom section of the VSM.

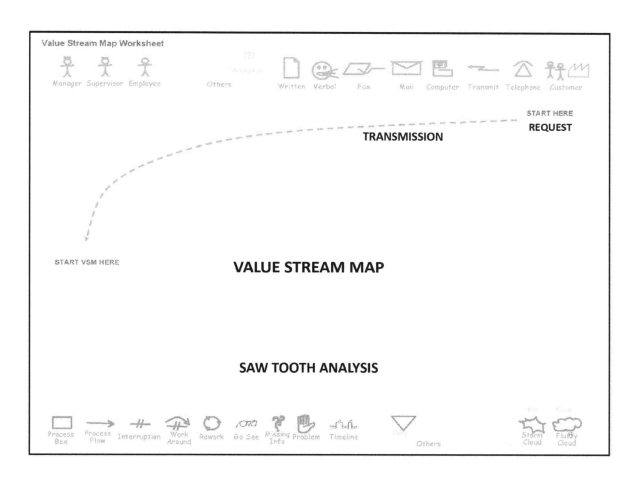

# Sample Value Stream Map Worksheet

**Value Stream Map Worksheet**

Manager Supervisor Employee

Others

Written Verbal Fax Mail Computer Transmit Telephone Customer

TRANSMISSION

START HERE

REQUEST

START VSM HERE

VALUE STREAM MAP

SAW TOOTH ANALYSIS

Process Box

Process Flow

Interruption

Work Around

Rework

Go See

Missing Info

Problem

Timeline

Storm Cloud

Fluffy Cloud

Others

# Understand the A3 Problem Solving Methodology

As discussed, A3 is a paper size (11 x 17 inches) that has been used for decades in what is now called A3 Problem Solving. The following sample worksheet is often preprinted, bound in a tablet to be distributed to promote simplicity and ease of use. Like the Value Stream Map, we suggest you use a pencil to do an A3 analysis so you can easily make changes.

## A3 Problem Solving Worksheet

| ISSUE: | FUTURE STATE: | TITLE: |
| --- | --- | --- |

To: ___
By: ___
Date: ___

BACKGROUND AND COSTS:

CURRENT STATE:

**A3 is a size of Paper (11" x 17")**
**A3 Problem Solving is the process on 11" x 17" Paper**

COUNTERMEASURES:

IMPLEMENTATION PLAN:

| WHAT: | WHO | WHEN | DONE? |
| --- | --- | --- | --- |

SITUATION ANALYSIS:

**Left Side of A3**          **Right Side of A3**

| IMPLEMENTATION COST | IMPLEMENTATION BENEFITS |
| --- | --- |

CHECK:

| FOLLOW-UP ACTIONS: | WHO | WHEN | DONE? |
| --- | --- | --- | --- |

GOALS AND TARGET:

6

The **left side** of the A3 worksheet is typically devoted to the **current state** process analysis. The **right side** is dedicated to the **future state** process analysis. Selected problem identification tools will be discussed later in this Concept. Other problem analysis tools will be covered later in the guide.

Note that traditional problem-solving methods and tools are employed for both process analysis and problem identification. However, by using the A3 worksheet, simplicity and ease of change are stressed. The process is deceptively easy to apply.

## The Traditional Problem-Solving Method, Steps, and Tools

- Clarify the goal, purpose or objective

- Define the problem or opportunity

- Gather facts and analyze (Gap Analysis)

- Generate alternatives and best solution

- Develop action plan and implement

- Follow-up and evaluate

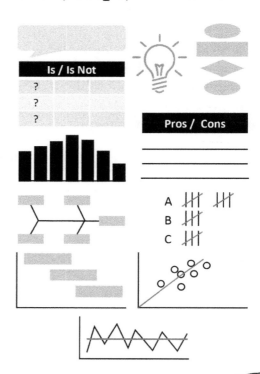

To improve any process, start by defining the current or as-is state of the process. As previously discussed, one of the first steps is to observe a process and diagram it in a flowchart or process map. After that, you can review problems and opportunities for improvement. As a caution, one of the mistakes often made is jumping ahead to try to improve a process without adequately observing and diagraming its current state.

Defining the problem, goal, and objective may sound easy, but be warned: **It is not**. It requires a commitment of thought, analysis, and time. People often identify symptoms of the problem and do not get to the root cause or causes.

Following is a template to use to help you more effectively **define a problem**.

## Example Format for Defining a Problem

Presently _____

that (or who) supplies _____

to _____

does not _____

which causes _____

and results in _____

Clearly defining the problem makes gathering facts, analyzing data, and generating alternatives a lot easier.

Below are some commonly used tools for solving problems, followed by a discussion of how they are typically employed.

### Common Tools Used in Problem Solving

**Team Dynamics**
- Brainstorming
- Nominal Group Techniques
- Force Field Analysis (Pro/Con)
- Stratification (Is/Is Not Matrix)

**Problem Identification**
- Check Sheets
- Flow Charts
- Pareto Charts
- Histograms
- Surveys

**Problem Analysis**
- Cause & Effect Diagrams
- Scatter Diagrams
- Run Charts
- Control Charts
- Gantt Charts

6

Previously we described the importance of observation and diagramming (using flowcharts and process maps) as tools in problem identification. Following are descriptions of some other commonly used **problem identification** tools.

**Check Sheets** – A check sheet is a simple data-collection tool used for recording data, such as the number of occurrences of an event. This is the most basic data-gathering tool, and it can be adapted to fit a wide range of situations. An Observation Worksheet may be one type of check sheet. Almost any worksheet or template used to collect or tally data in real time at the location where the data is generated (quantitative or qualitative) could be considered a check sheet.

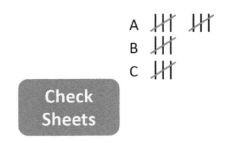

**Pareto Charts** – Named after Vilfredo Pareto, an Italian engineer and economist, a Pareto Chart is a type of chart that illustrates individual values in descending order (typically bars), and the line represents the cumulative total. This tool is particularly useful in determining what opportunities for improvement may be the best to explore first.

The Pareto chart also illustrates the Pareto Principle (the 80/20 rule) and shows you what processes are leading to most of your revenue, costs, results, problems, and so on. The idea is that 20 percent of activity accounts for 80 percent of productivity (as cited in Reh, n.d.), which is what a Pareto chart shows you. In other words, it shows you what processes accomplish the most. Knowing this can help you identify the best places to invest your time, money, and improvement efforts.

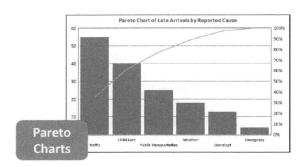

**Histograms** – In statistics, a histogram is a visual representation of the distribution of data. Histograms are used to plot density of data, and often for density estimation. For example, you might estimate the probability density function of the underlying variable.

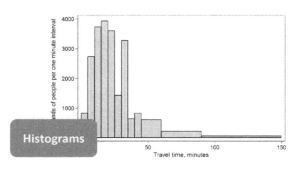

**Root Cause Analysis and 5 Whys** – The analysis of problems has shown that asking "Why?" five times will typically result in a solution. The resulting 5 Whys method is an iterative technique used to explore the cause of a problem. The five in the name derives from anecdotal observation about the number of iterations needed to resolve problems.

The primary technique is to determine the root cause or causes of a problem by repeating the question "Why?" However, it is often helpful to interchange Who, What, Where, and When for Why. Each answer forms the basis of the next question.

Here is a **famous example of 5 Whys and root cause analysis**:

The concrete was falling from a section of the Jefferson Memorial ceiling.

**Why**? It is being washed several times a week.

   **Why**? There are lots of pigeon droppings.

      **Why**? Pigeons come to eat the spiders.

         **Why**? Spiders come to eat the midges.

            **Why**? Midges fly to the floodlights of the monument.

               **Why**? The lights come on before dusk and attract the midges.

After you get to the root of a problem, the question becomes what are you going to do about it? What practical actions or countermeasures can be taken? What are your desired outcomes, realistic goals, and proposed actions for improving the situation and how can you know when you have achieved them?

**Surveys** – Most people have participated in surveys at one point or another. They are a method of collecting quantitative information about items in a population.

*Identify the actual problems*
*— process is taking too long*
*— no visibility after contract is signed*
*— need better Reporting*

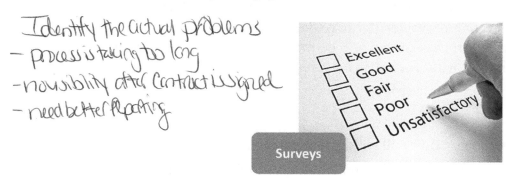

Surveys

6

## Process Improvement Case Study: Designing for Innovation

**Current State**: An organization realized that opportunities for innovation were typically discovered during the production phase, but this is when it is more expensive to implement changes. Further, beyond a suggestion box, the organization realized it did not have a transparent corporatewide innovation vetting process.

The leadership decided to set up an innovation team to identify and develop an innovation process. The team started by developing a series of flowcharts of how innovation currently was handled in each of the organization's major business units. They then focused on understanding the voids that existed and envisioned what a centralized strategic innovation process would look like.

**Future State**: The team advocated for formalizing the innovation process in each of its major business units' operational processes rather than an after-thought at the production phase. The business unit processes would be like what Toyota implemented whereby workers at different phases of the production process are empowered to stop production, fix issues, perform routine maintenance, and take steps to improve the processes. The team then developed a centralized corporate innovation process for vetting strategic initiatives considered beyond the scope of individual business units and included representatives from each business unit.

**Impact**: The streamlined innovation process provided transparency, had shorter chains of command, clearer roles and responsibilities, and most importantly allocated resources and timelines for innovation before and during pre-production. Staff could simultaneously focus on production as well as innovation that allows for iterative design and feedback. The centralized innovation process served as a coordinating and communication mechanism as well as a forum for vetting strategic corporate opportunities.

## WHAT TO DO:

- ☐ Focus on the part of a process that will yield the most significant benefits.
- ☐ Identify tools that may be useful and that will make your efforts at analyzing the root cause easier.
- ☐ Determine what tools you can apply to your improvement initiative.

Other actions:

☐ _____

☐ _____

☐ _____

✓ It is suggested that A3 Problem Solving (like the VSM) be completed using a pencil with an eraser to promote simplicity and ease of change.

✓ Employ traditional problem-solving methodologies and tools as appropriate.

Watch the five-minute review of Concept 6:

***Using A3 Problem Solving*** (2016)

(click on the image to launch video)

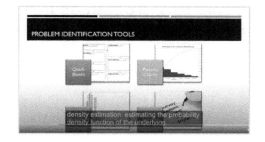

Visit the following link to and use the site's "A3 Navigation" functionality to learn more about structured A3 Problem Solving and how it is used in the healthcare industry. The site includes the steps for developing an A3 as well as a template and case study BY the College of Engineering - Montana State University.

***A3 Process*** (NSF Grant 2001)

Watch the following ten-minute video to learn more about A3 Problem:

***A3 Problem Solving Tool*** (2016)

Watch the following seven-minute video to learn more about A3 Problem Solving and gain an understanding of the key elements.

***A3 Problem Solving*** (2012)

Watch this two-minute video:

***QI Macros - Toyota A3 Report Template in Excel*** (2010)

6

**Reinforce Your Learning**

**Analyze the Current State (A3 - Left Side).** Review your **Value Stream Map** and identify what part of an improved process would result in the most significant positive results. Focus on that improvement and consider what tools may be useful in analyzing the current situation and how you might apply the tools to your improvement initiative. Use the left side of the A3 worksheet below or the A3 Problem Solving Worksheet available in Appendix E.

ISSUE:

FUTURE STATE:

TITLE:

To:

By:

BACKGROUND AND COSTS:

DATE:

CURRENT STATE:

## A3 is a size of Paper (11" x 17")
## A3 Problem Solving is the process on 11" x 17" Paper

COUNTERMEASURES:

IMPLEMENTATION PLAN:

| WHAT: | | WHO | WHEN | DONE? |
|---|---|---|---|---|

SITUATION ANALYSIS:

## Left Side of A3

## Right Side of A3

| IMPLEMENTATION COST | IMPLEMENTATION BENEFITS |
|---|---|

CHECK:

| FOLLOW-UP ACTIONS: | WHO | WHEN | DONE? |
|---|---|---|---|

GOALS AND TARGET:

6

## A3 Worksheet Planning (Current State, Left Side)

**Issue**: Identify the current state problem or need.

_____

_____

_____

_____

_____

**Background and Costs**: Conduct research to understand the current situation and describe costs and opportunities for improvement.

_____

_____

_____

_____

_____

**Current State**: Identify what parts of a process or sub-process – if improved – would result in the most significant impact. Insert that part from the Value Stream Map here.

_____

_____

_____

_____

_____

_____

_____

_____

6

**Situation Analysis**: Consider what tools may be useful in conducting a root cause analysis. List the tools here. For example, you might consider using Brainstorming, the 5 Whys, a Pareto diagram, or a Fishbone diagram, which is discussed in the next Concept.

_____

_____

_____

_____

_____

_____

**Goals and Target**: Describe the desired outcome, goals, and the recommended future state. Be as specific as practical, keeping in mind that a goal is a general area of improvement like reducing defects, improving quality, shortening cycle time, reducing costs, and so on. However, a target is the specific measure such as "Reduce defects by 10 percent within three months."

_____

_____

_____

_____

_____

_____

_____

_____

_____

_____

_____

_____

_____

_____

6

*It is possible to fly without motors, but not without knowledge and skill.*

– Wilbur Wright

# Apply Tools for Analyzing the Current Situation

Before you can improve a process by looking for solutions, you must first analyze the current state and its problem areas, possible barriers to improvement, and potential challenges and opportunities.

You must view the current situation from the customer's perspective. The Value-Stream Map will show the value that the customer places on the product or services flow. Ask this question: What is most valued by the customer? Price? Quality? Delivery? Response Time? Something else?

*[handwritten margin note: In Burlington's situation, the Customer would be our business partner. Could also be the Vendor?]*

Focus on the customer and potential barriers and challenges for improving the current state process, and then **brainstorm** potential problems, barriers, and challenges that could be preventing the process from being the best it could be.

**Brainstorming** is a process improvement tool developed by Alex Osborn. It has these four rules:

1. Focus on quantity.

2. Withhold criticism.

3. Welcome unusual ideas.

4. Combine and improve ideas.

Brainstorming is an intense activity, and after approximately five minutes some participants may become distracted and disengage. Virtual brainstorming can also be used quite effectively.

Structuring a brainstorming session can help make it more productive. Give participants clear instructions to focus on the process or topic at hand, remind everyone of the rules, and have someone document the ideas discussed.

Using a Brainstorming Worksheet, shown in the example below, is a good way to document a session and will pay dividends to the leader of the session. A Brainstorming Worksheet is available in Appendix F.

7

After the brainstorming session, you can categorize the input into themes and use the result for further analysis.

If you do not identify specific themes, you can sort almost any process into one of these standard categories: people, methods or procedures, materials, and machines or equipment.

**Brainstorming Worksheet**

| Category? | Barriers and Challenges |
|---|---|
| | 1. |
| | 2. |
| | 3. |
| | 4. |
| | 5. |
| | 6. |
| | 7. |

Categorize the brainstorming responses into relevant themes (or use the standard categories of people, methods or procedures, materials, machinery or equipment), and then consolidate and refine the listing under each category.

| Category? | Barriers and Challenges |
|---|---|
| | 1. |
| | 2. |
| | 3. |
| | 4. |
| | 5. |
| | 6. |
| | 7. |

When complete, categorize each idea as either:

A = People
B = Methods / Procedures
C = Materials
D = Machinery / Equipment

**Nominal Group Technique** – This technique allows a group to quickly prioritize many issues, concerns, or improvement ideas using a weighted ranking. Ask each person in the brainstorming group to select their top three choices from whatever list they generated. Then ask each participant to prioritize 1, 2, and 3, and then assign 5 points to their first choice, 3 points to their second choice, and 1 point to their third choice. Then go through the list and ask for the number of points each person assigned to each item. Finally, tally the totals for each item.

**Force Field Analysis** – A Force Field Analysis can be thought of as a prioritized pro and con diagram where the Driving Forces (Pro) and the Restraining Forces (Con) associated with an event are often displayed in descending balance sheet "T-Account" format. The analysis is useful for focusing a group on the most significant items.

**Stratification** – Stratification is the process of classifying data into subgroups or categories (Is / Is Not Matrix). As previously stated, a common stratification method used for analyzing a listing of potential problem causes (or barriers and challenges) is to categorize (or stratify) them into one of four major areas: people, methods or procedures, materials, machinery or equipment.

| Category | Is | Is not | So...(Conclusion) |
|---|---|---|---|
| People | | | |
| Methods | | | |
| Procedures | | | |
| Materials | | | |
| Machinery / Equipment | | | |

**Cause and Effect** – Cause and Effect is a diagramming tool commonly used to analyze potential barriers and challenges to improvement efforts. It is called an Ishikawa diagram after its creator but is also referred to a Fishbone diagram. The tool is frequently used in Lean efforts to identify potential factors causing an overall effect.

For purposes of our analysis, each cause or reason is a potential barrier or challenge to achieving the goal of having the best process. Below is an example of a completed Cause and Effect diagram with input gleaned from brainstorming the barriers and challenges of making toast. A Cause and Effect Diagram Worksheet is available in Appendix G.

7

## Barriers and Challenges of Making Toast Using a Cause and Effect Diagram

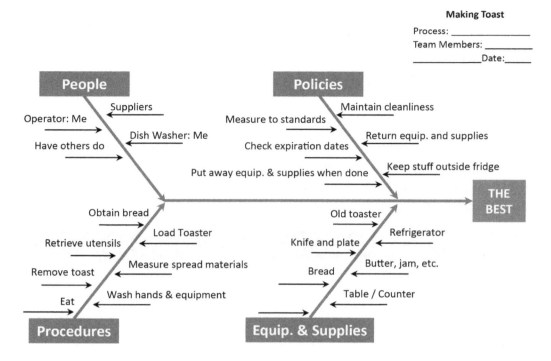

After **brainstorming** possible barriers and challenges, categorizing and consolidating responses, and entering rational responses on the Cause and Effect diagram, you will be ready to review selected areas via a Root Cause analysis, which is often called the **5 Whys**, as previously discussed.

| 5 Why's – Problem Solving |
|---|
| The toast is burnt... |
| Your car won't start... |
| Your report or proposal is late.... |
| • Why? |
| • Why? |
| • Why? |

After you find the root cause or causes, the question becomes what are you going to do about it? What practical actions or countermeasures can you take? What are realistic goals for improving the situation and how can you know when you have achieved them?

**Scatter Diagrams** – A Scatter diagram is typically used to view the possible relationship between one variable and another. On a Scatter diagram (also referred to as Scatter Plot), data is displayed as a collection of points, each having the value of one variable determining the position on the horizontal axis and the value of the other variable determining the position on the vertical axis. This tool, like the Run Chart below, is most often used in Six Sigma efforts.

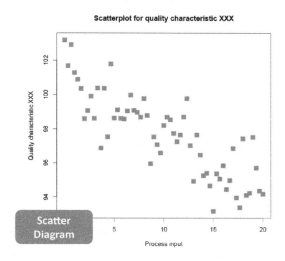

**Run Charts** – A Run Chart is typically used to visually represent data and to analyze and monitor a process to determine whether it is changing. Run Charts display data in a time sequence. The data displayed often represents an aspect of output or the performance of a business process.

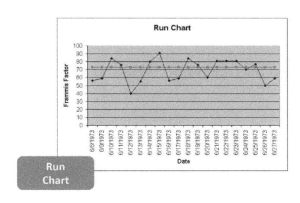

7

## Process Improvement Case Study: Improve Patient Scheduling

**Current State**: Upon arrival for a doctor's appointment, patients had to wait in line to be checked in by the receptionist, who would then proceed to ask a series of redundant questions about address, insurance coverage, and emergency contact, which sometimes caused delays. The long lines were often a source of customer complaints expressed in post-appointment surveys.

**Future State**: To speed the process and reduce lines, staff and leadership established a voluntary process improvement team that observed the situation, reviewed survey data, brainstormed solutions, and benchmarked organizations with similar issues. One initiative they recommended focused on implementing self-service kiosks as a way for patients to complete the check in process quickly and privately.

**Impact**: With more than one kiosk available, patients can check in for appointments without waiting in long lines. This has helped reduce patient waiting and increased customer satisfaction, which was reflected in post-appointment surveys.

### What To Do:

☐ Brainstorm the barriers and challenges of your problematic process.

☐ Categorize and consolidate the ideas generated by employing the four primary categories (people, methods, materials, and machines), or other categories as appropriate.

☐ Input the categorized ideas into the Cause and Effect diagram.

Other actions:

7

☐ _____

☐ _____

☐ _____

**Remember**

✓ Brainstorming, Cause and Effect diagrams, and Root Cause analysis are commonly used tools that will help you analyze a problem or situation. They are deceptively easy to apply.

✓ The keys to effective brainstorming are as follows: focus initially on quantity, not quality, withhold criticism or judgment, welcome unusual ideas, conclude by combining and improving the listing of ideas.

✓ The causes of almost any problem can be placed into four major categories on a Cause and Effect diagram: people, methods or procedures, materials, machinery or equipment.

✓ To get to the root cause of almost any problem ask "Why" five times. Of course, you may get to the root by asking "Why" (or Who, What, Where, When) two or three times, or it may take five or six times. It is not as difficult as you may think to get to the root cause of various problems. Ask yourself a question such as, "Why am I stressed?" and see the process in action.

**Enhance Your Learning**

Watch the nine-minute review of Concept 7:

***Applying Tools for Evaluating the Current Situation*** (2016)

(click on the image to launch video)

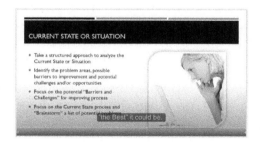

Visit the following link to see a three-minute video about how to brainstorm:

***Brainstorming | Structured brainstorming*** (2020)

7

Watch the following seven-minute video which overviews Cause and Effect diagrams and how you can use them to establish the root cause of problems:

*Fishbone Diagram Explained with Example* (2020)

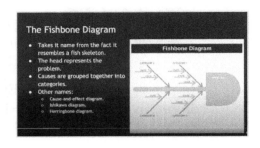

Watch the following three-minute video to learn more about the 5 Whys Technique, a simple way of getting to the root of problems:

*The 5 Whys - Lean Problem Solving* (2018)

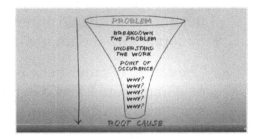

**Reinforce Your Learning**

**Brainstorming and Developing a Cause and Effect Diagram**. For the process you identified as the focus for applying Lean tools and methodologies, do the following:

1. Brainstorm the barriers and challenges of your process.

2. Categorize the ideas using the four categories indicated (see the example below).

3. Consolidate the ideas using the Cause and Effect analysis.

4. Copy the Cause and Effect diagram into the Situational Analysis section of the A3 Worksheet (left side), or if appropriate incorporate your 5 Why's analysis.

5. Analyze the root cause or causes of the important components of the Cause and Effect diagram and subsequently formulate your desired outcomes and improvement goals. Then insert the goals into the Goals and Target section of the A3 Worksheet (left side).

# A3 Worksheet (left side)

**+ Issue**

**+ Background and Costs**

**+ Current State**

**+ Situation Analysis**: Insert selected parts from the completed Cause and Effect diagram and/or the 5 Why's Analysis.

**+ Goals and Target**: From your Root Cause analysis, translate your possible actions or countermeasures into practical improvement targets.

| ISSUE: |
| --- |
| BACKGROUND AND COSTS: |
| CURRENT STATE: |
| SITUATION ANALYSIS: |
| GOALS AND TARGET: |

## Summary of Steps for Brainstorming and Categorizing Barriers and Challenges

Here is a summary of the steps for categorizing ideas from a brainstorming session.

1. Take five minutes and brainstorm barriers and challenges that may get in the way of solving the issue or problem you are studying and record them. Eliminate duplicates and consolidate the ideas from the brainstorming sessions into a master list.

7

| Category? | Barriers and Challenges |
|---|---|
| | 1. |
| | 2. |
| | 3. |
| | 4. |
| | 5. |
| | 6. |
| | 7. |
| | 8. |
| | 9. |
| | 10. |
| | 11. |
| | 12. |
| | 13. |
| | 14. |
| | 15. |
| | 16. |
| | 17. |
| | 18. |
| | 19. |
| | 20. |
| | 21. |
| | 22. |
| | 23. |
| | 24. |
| | 25. |

7

2. Assign a category to each idea using one of the following categories: A = People, B=Methods, C=Materials, D=Machines. Enter the letter A, B, C, or D in the left column, as shown below. Some ideas may fit into more than one category.

| Category? | Barriers and Challenges |
|---|---|
| 1. | |
| 2. | When complete, categorize each idea as either: |
| 3. | A = People |
| 4. | B = Methods / Procedures |
| | C = Materials |
| 5. | D = Machinery / Equipment |
| 6. | |
| 7. | |

3. Consolidate the ideas and add them to the Cause and Effect diagram.

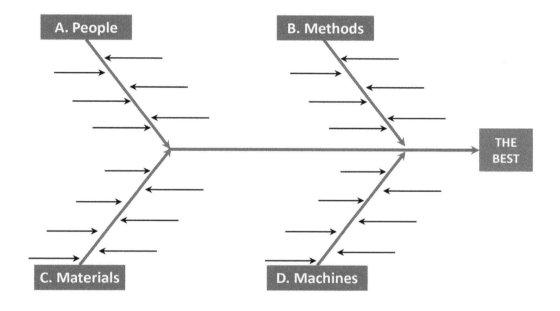

4. Copy the Cause and Effect diagram into the Situational Analysis section of the A3 Worksheet (left side)

5. Analyze the root cause or causes of the important components of the Cause and Effect diagram and then determine your desired outcomes and improvement goals. Enter the goals in the Goals and Target section of the A3 Worksheet (left side).

7

*Plans are nothing: planning is everything.*

– Dwight D. Eisenhower

# Apply Tools for Future State Planning

Once you understand the current situation and ideas about potential actions or countermeasures to improve the current process, you can use various tools to do future state planning. The focus of future state planning is not on an ideal state but rather an improved future state.

Future State Map and Future State Planning

- A future state map is a graphical representation of what the desired new process should look like
- Use a pencil so you can easily make modifications
- Not ideal, but brings you closer
- Is created by the team
- View how the current state is transformed into the A3 future state

Future State Plan

- Moves the A3 from current state to future state
- Considers target and goals
- At least one countermeasure for each root cause
- Countermeasures are the basis for implementation planning

The first step in any future state planning is to reach consensus on what the desired future state should look like. After that, you can transfer a sketch to the A3 Worksheet, as illustrated below.

8

## Desired Future State Layout of Work Area for Making Toast

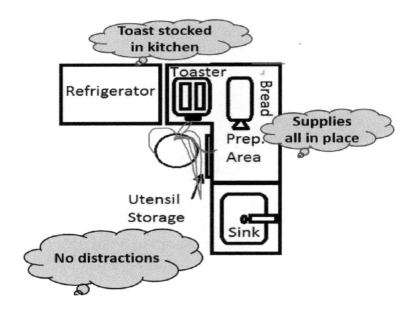

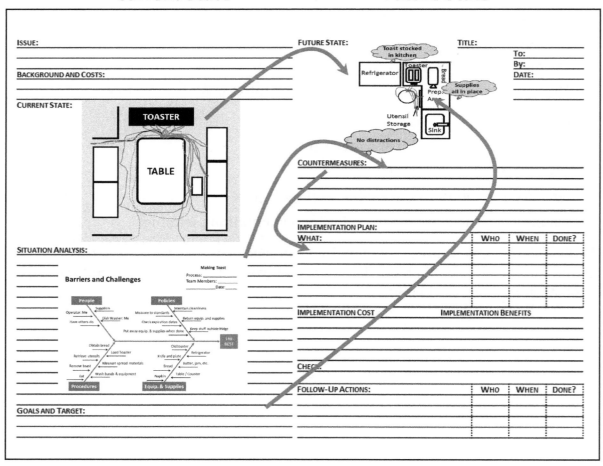

Common tools for future state planning and completion of the right side of an A3 Worksheet include:

- 5S Tools and methodology
- Standardized Work Plans, Visual Management, Just-In-Time (JIT) inventory planning
- Implementation planning
- Cost-Benefit Analysis
- Follow-up plans

**5S Methodology** – You may have considered the components of the 5S methodology when analyzing the current state of the process. Now that you have moved to the desired future state, it is time to document what actions you may want to implement. Use the right side of the A3 Worksheet to document the actions.

5S is a series of tools and a method used by organizations to organize a workplace, especially a **shared** workplace, like an office or shop floor. It is much more than housekeeping. It aims to improve workplace efficiency, morale, and safety. Assigning everything **that is needed** to a specific location saves time hunting things down and shows when something is missing from its designated location.

**The 5S's**

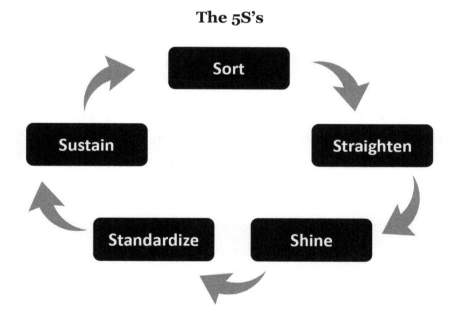

Three other S's are sometimes included: Safety, Security, and Satisfaction.

Following are descriptions of what to do to satisfy each of the 5S's:

**5S – Sort**

☐ Take stock of inventory in the work area.

☐ Get rid of all non-essential items.

☐ Keep regularly needed items close and easily accessible.

☐ Put less needed items further away or higher up.

☐ Free up storage space.

Questions to ask about each item:
- Useable or not useable?
- Essential, wanted, or unwanted?
- Current or obsolete?
- Used frequently or infrequently?
- Better stored somewhere else?

**5S – Straighten**

☐ Organize and label locations for all items. Keep items used most often closest, less used items further away, and rarely used items stored even farther away. Also, include symbols, graphics, and photographs showing the progression from a non-5S area to a 5S area.

**5S – Shine**

☐ Clean the workspace.

☐ Ensure each piece of equipment is clean and in working order.

☐ Start with the main work area and work out from there.

☐ All materials needed for work are available and marked.

**5S – Standardize**

☐ Develop procedures for cleaning and re-stocking the work area.
  – Methods
  – Standards
  – Schedule

☐ Assign responsibilities.

☐ Post expectations.

**5S – Sustain**

☐ Review the workplace regularly.

8

☐ Consider starting with the sort step each time a product change occurs or when new materials or forms are added to the inventory.

☐ Audit regularly and post scores.

☐ Plan and give assignments for maintaining and improving the area.

## 5S Example: Making Toast

### Sort

- Place utensils in proper locations before and after use.
- Place bread in breadbox or drawer.

### Straighten

- Place bread, plates, and utensils needed close to toaster.
- Place butter, jam, and all other items in proper place in refrigerator.
- Label and orient items so that they can be easily viewed.

### Shine: Cleanliness

- Prepare on plates.
- Fasten material lids.
- Keep work area clean.
- Load plates into the dishwasher after use.
- Wash directly after use.
- Plate and knife.

### Standardize: Measurements

- ½ ounce of materials each
- Temperature: Calibrate in advance
- Type of bread: white, wheat, and so on
- Time: Consistent attention
- Process order: Maintain sequential task order

### Sustain: Commit

- Maintain standardization
- Long term: Efficient equipment
- Recyclable materials

8

The following page shows the 5S Assessment Worksheet. A 5S Assessment Worksheet is also available in Appendix H.

### Sample 5S Assessment Worksheet

**5S Assessment**

Organization / Work Area: _____

By: _____ Date: _____

*Instructions: Next to each statement, check the number (1 to 5) that indicates your level of agreement with the statement, with 1 being **strongly disagree** and 5 being **strongly agree**. When finished total your ratings.*

| | | | 1 | 2 | 3 | 4 | 5 |
|---|---|---|---|---|---|---|---|
| **SORT** (Seiri) | | Procedures are established and evident. Every item in the area is needed for regular work. No extraneous items are found in any area location. Only the minimum standard amount of inventory and supplies are in the area. | | | | | |
| **STRAIGHTEN** (Seiton) | | All items have a specific location and in their proper place. Area is very well organized with regularly used items stored in designated convenient locations. Excellent visual controls are in evidence. | | | | | |
| **SHINE** (Seiso) | | Equipment, work surfaces and storage areas are clean. Every item in the area is in "like new" condition. The area is thoroughly cleaned on a regular basis and is kept in a spotless condition. | | | | | |
| **STANDARDIZE** (Seiketsu) | | Specific organizing tasks have been assigned for the work area with responsibilities clearly noted. There is an up-to-work area layout diagram, duty list, and schedule posted. There is evidence that duties are done regularly. | | | | | |
| **SUSTAIN** (Shitsuke) | | Everyone is involved in improvement activities and all levels of the organization are dedicated to sustaining the 5S program. There is regular leadership participation in reviews. All areas are "audit ready" at all times. | | | | | |
| | | **TOTAL RATING (Add Values)** | | | | | |

### Standardized Work Plans, Visual Management, JIT, and Countermeasures

Standard work is typically the most effective combination of people, materials, and equipment. Creating a Standard Work Plan is a method whereby you focus on continuously improving the major categories or elements of the Cause and Effect diagram – people, materials, equipment, and methods – until you achieve the most effective or standard situation.

Once you have developed a Standard Work Plan, use the Observation Worksheet (or adapt your own version) to document the process. It may also serve as a way for you to communicate process ideas to management.

### Standardized Work Plans / Visual Management / JIT / Countermeasures

*Standard work* is typically the most effective combination of people, materials, and equipment. Creating a Standard Work Plan is a method whereby you typically focus on continuously improving the major categories or elements of the Cause and Effect diagram: people, materials, equipment, and methods until the most effective or standard is achieved.

Once you have established a Standard Work Plan, you can use, or adapt, the Observation Worksheet previously discussed to document the process. It may also serve as a Visual Management tool for the new Standard Work Plan and for implementing Just-In-Time (JIT) inventory strategies where appropriate.

### ✳ Standard Work Plan

- Visually shows the steps in order and their time.

- Can show additional information about the work being performed.

- A Standard Work Plan Worksheet is available in Appendix I.

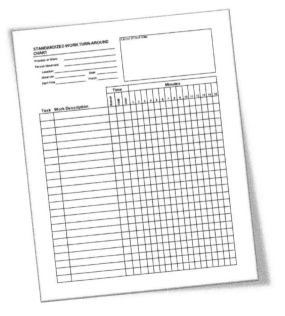

Sometimes countermeasures are needed to implement work plans or other future state implementation plans. A *countermeasure* is an action taken to prevent an undesirable outcome. Countermeasures can also be proactive actions to achieve your objectives.

## Implementation Planning

Implementation planning in the context of Lean and A3 Problem Solving are plans that provide sufficient cost-benefit detail and action planning steps to successfully transition the process from the current state to the desired future state.

Implementation planning typically involves identifying the following kinds of information:

- What actions or steps need to happen?
- Who will do them?
- When will they be completed?
- How much will the improvement initiative cost?
- What are the benefits?
- What follow-up actions are appropriate?

Following are examples of the Value Stream Maps for both the Current and Future State processes for Making Toast, and the case studies introduced in Concept 5: Select the Cheaper Hotel, and Streamline Proposal Process.

## Example 1: Current and Future State Value Stream Maps for Making Toast

Current VSM

Overall: 5 min 55 sec.
Avg. Wait: 55 sec.
Avg. Process: 5 min

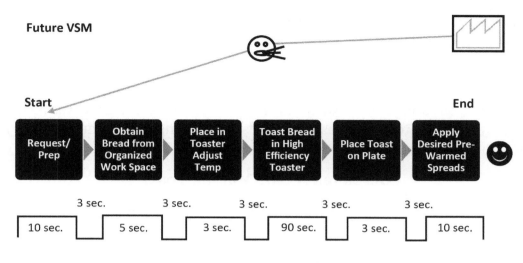

Future VSM

Start ... End

| Request/ Prep | Obtain Bread from Organized Work Space | Place in Toaster Adjust Temp | Toast Bread in High Efficiency Toaster | Place Toast on Plate | Apply Desired Pre-Warmed Spreads |

3 sec.   3 sec.   3 sec.   3 sec.   3 sec.

10 sec.   5 sec.   3 sec.   90 sec.   3 sec.   10 sec.

Overall: 2 min 15 sec. (-3 min. 39 sec.)
Avg. Wait: 15 sec. (-40 sec.)
Avg. Process: 2 min. 1 sec. (-2 min. 59 sec.)

### Cost-Benefit Analysis for Making Toast (Current versus Future Process)

- Excess motion reduced from 45 seconds to 6 seconds: 87% improvement
- Extra processing step eliminated
- Conventional way versus 5S way: from 355 seconds to 136 seconds (62% improvement)
- Jam: $4.19 for 12oz versus $0.17 for 1/2oz
- Butter: $2.29 for 8oz versus $0.15oz for 1/2oz

### A3 Problem Solving Worksheet

The **A3 Problem Solving Worksheet** can often add structure to an analysis, and it typically is used as a primary document to communicate with decision makers. It conveys a succinct picture of both the current state and the proposed future state. As such, you have a decision to make as to what tools are most relevant and impactful to display in your completed document.

Below are some A3 examples. For clarity, the examples have been segmented into the left side (Current State) and the right side (Future State) views of a typical A3 worksheet.

For the making toast example, we could display the Current and Future State Value Stream Maps; however, in this case, we decided the Current and Future State workflow and the Spaghetti diagram may be more impactful.

As for the Situation Analysis, we could simply narratively describe the situation and our thoughts or display our 5Why's analysis. However, in this case, we decided to include our Cause and Effect Diagram. It offers a variety of possible factors that could potentially affect the time it takes to make toast and that people may tend to overlook.

For our Cost-Benefit analysis, we could focus on various costs. However, in this case, the most important factor is probably wait time, especially if someone is in a hurry to get to work. For our analysis, the **bottom line** is that the overall time was reduced from 5 min 55 seconds to 2 minutes 15 seconds for a savings of 3 minutes and 39 seconds with no implementation cost.

## Completed A3 for Making Toast

Left Side of A3                    Right Side of A3

## Current State                    Future State

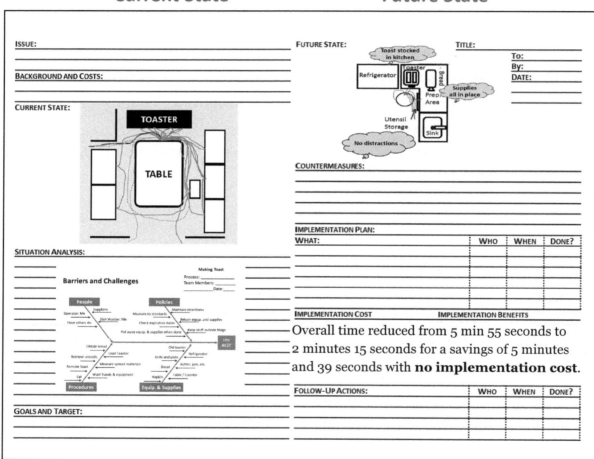

The following examples are a continuat of the case studies introduced in Concept 5.

## Example 2: Select the Cheaper Hotel? (Current State - Left Side of A3)

**Issue**: Didn't maximize time and networking opportunities at conference/ tradeshow due to travel delays and logistical challenges primarily due to hotel location and distance from the conference.

**Background and Costs**: Due to financial constraints, a lower cost hotel was booked that was further away from the conference/tradeshow. While the hotel saved $50, additional travel time and transportation costs were required.

**Current State**:

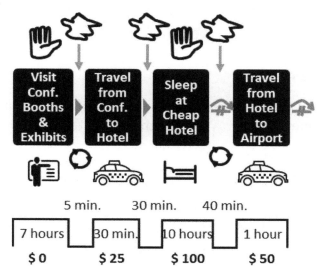

**Situation Analysis**:

The location of the hotel was several miles beyond the location of the conference and in the opposite direction of the airport. It was $50 cheaper to stay there instead of the $150 per night hotel that was closer and within walking distance. However the travel time and travel costs made the situation inconvenient. Additionally, due to the extra distance and extra taxi cab requirements it made attending evening networking/vendor gatherings unattractive.

**Goals and Targets**:

To reduce travel time and total costs and maximize time available to attend conference/tradeshow sessions and networking events.

8

## Example 2: Select the Cheaper Hotel? (Future State - Right Side of A3)

**Future State**:

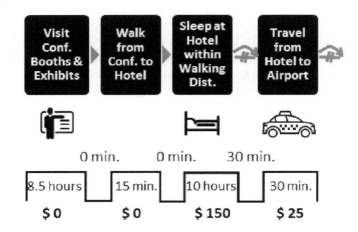

**Countermeasures**:

Book a hotel near to the conference and within walking distance of the conference center instead of one miles away and further from the airport.

**Implementation Plan**:

+ Research early hotel options and book a hotel within walking distance
+ Obtain conference program ahead of time and i Identify and prioritize conference sessions to attend
+ Develop a map of which exhibits to visit
+ Identify networking / vendor events and logistical considerations
+ Explore mass-transit options to/from airport

**Implementation Cost**:

+ Extra $50 for hotel

**Implementation Benefits**:

+ Saved $50 in transportation costs
+ Saved 1 hr. 30 min in travel time permitting more time at conference
+ Able to attend evening receptions/networking/vendor events
+ More relaxed / less stress and hassle

**Check**: Ask colleagues what they liked best and worst

**Follow Up Actions**: Re-evaluate trip plans and apply learning to next trip

From our analysis, the **bottom line** is that overall, it is cost-effective and better to select the higher priced hotel within walking distance to the conference site.

## Example 3: Streamline Proposal Process (Current State - Left Side of A3)

**Issue**: Kill bad projects early. Expedited preliminary "Go/No GO" review process to determine merits of pursuing further analysis leading to formal proposal efforts.

Background and Costs: Multiple requests made within short "windows of opportunity" require appropriate people to review and appraise potential benefit/cost associated with new programs/projects.

**Current State**:

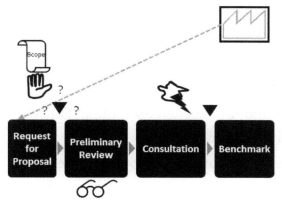

**Situation Analysis**:

**Goals and Targets**: One week turnaround of preliminary review. Vet concepts and reach consensus on whether to proceed further (Go/ No Go Decision) in an objective & expedited way priorto investing additional scarce operational resources.

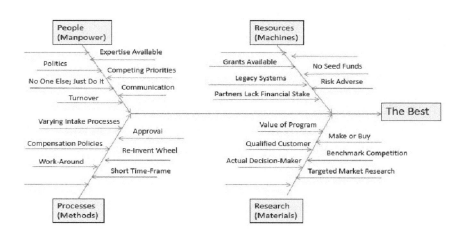

8

## Example 3: Streamline Proposal Process (Future State - Right Side of A3)

**Future State**:

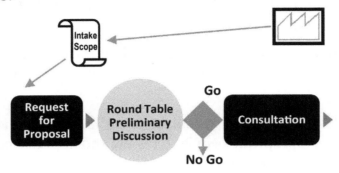

**Countermeasures**:

Develop preliminary "Intake Form/Project Scope" criteria and preliminary project review process

**Implementation Plan**:

+ Develop criteria and info needed for "Intake Form"
+ Identify stakeholders and solicit input
+ Create database and/or project log book process
+ Develop preliminary project proposal plan process template
+ Pilot the process and adjust accordingly

**Implementation Cost**:

+ Staff Time of $5K + 5K for software = $10 K

**Implementation Benefits**:

Assume save 5 days/project @ $1000/day x 10 projects = $50K

**Check**: Pilot test for 3 months

**Follow Up Actions**: Re-evaluate pilot in 3 months

From our analysis, the **bottom line** is that considerable savings in time and money can be achieved by assembling and soliciting preliminary input from key stakeholders at the early proposal stage to determine Go/No go before investing in a detailed analysis.

## Process Improvement Case Study: Do Not Reinvent the Wheel

**Current State**: In one large organization, non-standard production worksheets created product and service inconsistencies, which resulted in increased errors, defects, scrap, and lack of accountability.

**Future State**: Standardized step by step process worksheets for each piece of equipment prevented individuals from re-inventing the wheel. Developing detailed user guides and job aids also helped individuals troubleshoot issues. The standardized worksheets and job aids are now being used to design a next-generation augmented-reality maintenance approach.

**Impact**: Minimized downtime, increased production efficiency, reduced waste and down time, improved quality, and documented standard methods, procedures, and work plans.

## WHAT TO DO:

☐ Sketch the desired future state of your problematic process.

☐ Determine how you will implement the 5S's to improve and sustain planned actions.

☐ Develop a Standard Work Plan by outlining the steps and timing of your future state.

Other actions:

☐ _____

☐ _____

☐ _____

8

**Remember**

✓ The focus of future state planning is not necessarily on an *ideal* state but rather on achieving an *improved* state.

✓ The tools for future state planning can be deceptively simple to implement and are often overlooked or ignored. However, it is not what you call them that counts, but why and how you employ them, and the results you obtain, that matter.

 **Enhance Your Learning**

Watch the nine-minute review of Concept 8:

***Applying Tools for Future State Planning*** (2016)

(click on the image to launch video)

Watch the following six-minute video focused on 5S Methodology:

***Introduction to 5S Methodology Training - Lean Manufacturing Principles*** (2019)

Watch the four-minute video to obtain an overview of standardized work:

***Lean Manufacturing - Standardized Work*** (2020)

8

Then watch the two-minute video to view the use of simple standard work visual tools in a production environment:

***Lean Manufacturing Standard Work Made Simple*** (2019)

Watch the four-minute video to learn more about Just In Time (JIT) production from the best:

***Just in Time by Toyota: The Smartest Production System in The World*** (2017)

8

**Reinforce Your Learning**

**A3 Future State Planning – Standard Work Plan**. For the process you identified as the focus for applying Lean tools and methodologies, consider what tools are appropriate for the right side of the A3 worksheet. Then using the Standard Work Plan Worksheet that follows, insert, or sketch the layout of your future work process or layout of work area. Then list the standard work elements and the target timeframe for each element. A Standard Work Plan Worksheet is also available in Appendix I.

**Standard Work Plan**

Process or Sub-Process: _____

Layout of Work Area: Begin by sketching a layout of the desired work area below.

8

List the standard work elements and the target timeframe associated with each element.

| Work Elements | | TIME | | | Minutes | | | | | | | | | |
| Task # | Description | Work | Travel | Wait | 1 | 2 | 3 | 4 | 5 | 6 | 7 | 8 | 9 | 10 |
|---|---|---|---|---|---|---|---|---|---|---|---|---|---|---|
| | | | | | | | | | | | | | | |
| | | | | | | | | | | | | | | |
| | | | | | | | | | | | | | | |
| | | | | | | | | | | | | | | |
| | | | | | | | | | | | | | | |
| | | | | | | | | | | | | | | |
| | | | | | | | | | | | | | | |
| | | | | | | | | | | | | | | |
| | | | | | | | | | | | | | | |
| | | | | | | | | | | | | | | |
| | | | | | | | | | | | | | | |
| | | | | | | | | | | | | | | |
| | | | | | | | | | | | | | | |
| | | | | | | | | | | | | | | |
| | | | | | | | | | | | | | | |
| | | | | | | | | | | | | | | |
| | | | | | | | | | | | | | | |
| | | | | | | | | | | | | | | |
| | | | | | | | | | | | | | | |
| | | | | | | | | | | | | | | |

8

*Without a standard, there is no logical basis for decision making or taking action.*

– Joseph M. Juran

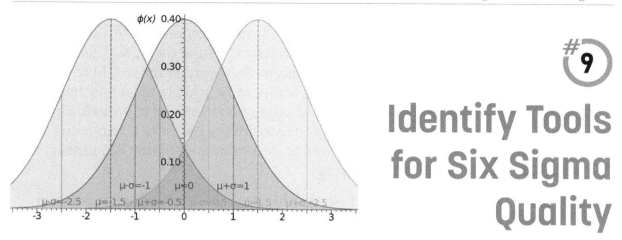

# Identify Tools for Six Sigma Quality

**Six Sigma** uses statistical concepts and methodologies initially adopted by Motorola. Organizations use Six Sigma to guide them through the steps of continuous improvement, which includes reducing variation, eliminating defects, and perfecting processes.

Six Sigma is typically a top-down methodology. That means the decision to pursue various initiatives comes from the top of the organization or the leadership of a business unit. For project success, Six Sigma requires a commitment of people, time, and other necessary resources.

## Resources, Training, and Approach to Six Sigma

The challenges and opportunities are enormous, and the resources and training supporting the use of Six Sigma are unprecedented. Some of the world's leading organizations have organized their Six Sigma initiatives and talent resources into five categories

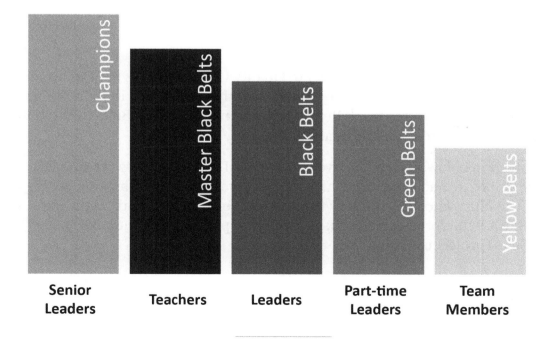

9

✳ **Champions** – These are senior management leaders responsible for the success of the Six Sigma efforts. Champions approve projects, fund them, and alleviate roadblocks to project success. Some business leaders are champions. Most champions directly report to the business leader. A typical business may have seven to ten champions. The champions should reflect a mix of transaction and production process improvement targets needed in the business. Champions do not need to be full-time, but they do need to devote whatever time is necessary to ensure that their projects are successful.

✳ **Master Black Belts** – First and foremost Master Black Belts must be teachers. They review and mentor Black Belts, and these are typically full-time jobs. Selection criteria for Master Black Belts are quantitative skills and the ability to teach and mentor.

**Black Belts** – These are the leaders of teams responsible for measuring, analyzing, improving, and controlling key processes that influence customer satisfaction and productivity growth. Black Belts are typically full-time positions.

**Green Belts** – Green Belts are trained by a similar method as Black Belts, but they usually stay in their operating assignments and work Six Sigma projects part-time, typically as team leaders or members.

**Yellow Belts** – Typically these are team members or others associated in some way with Six Sigma projects. As such, they support the goals of the project, and usually in the context of their existing responsibilities. They must understand the overall concepts and terminology of Six Sigma. After participating in a Six Sigma project, Yellow Belts are expected to continue using Six Sigma tools as part of regular jobs.

Champions and Master Black Belts are trained on the Six Sigma approach: Champions ask the right questions. Master Black Belts teach and mentor. This is true for manufacturing as well as service-related leaders.

Once a project is identified, the Critical to Quality Characteristics (CTQs) are defined. This is the first step in the process. Then the other steps in the Six Sigma methodology begin. Master Black Belts guide and mentor Black Belts through the next phases, which are measure, analyze, improve, and control.

The illustration below depicts the five steps of the DMAIC process (**D**efine, **M**easure, **A**nalyze, **I**mprove, and **C**ontrol), which are the same steps for achieving Six Sigma quality. The illustration also depicts the knowledge domains of Six Sigma and Lean Sigma: Black Belts (project leaders); Green Belts (project team members); and Yellow Belts (project contributors).

9

## Six Sigma Process Improvement Cycle™

**Six-Sigma 5 Steps**

1. Define
2. Measure
3. Analyze
4. Improve
5. Control

★ **Define**: The objective of this step is to describe the context in which the Six Sigma project is performed.

★ **Measure**: The objectives of this step are to identify the key internal processes that influence CTQs and measure the defects generated relative to identified CTQs. A CTQ may be defined as a feature of a product or service that is considered critical to the customer. Defects are defined as out-of-tolerance CTQs. The end of this phase occurs when the Black Belt can successfully measure the defects generated for a key process affecting the CTQ.

★ **Analyze**: The objective of this step is to understand why defects are generated. Brainstorming, statistical tools, and so on are used to identify key variables (Xs) that cause defects. The output of this phase is an explanation of the variables that are likely to drive process variation the most.

★ **Improve**: The objectives of this step are to confirm the key variables, quantify the effect of these variables on the CTQs, identify the maximum acceptable ranges of the key variables, ensure that the measurement systems are capable of measuring the key variables, and modify the process to stay within acceptable ranges.

★ **Control**: The objective of this step is to ensure that the modified process now enables the key variables (Xs) to stay within the maximum acceptable ranges using tools such as statistical process control (SPC) or checklists.

As previously discussed, **Lean** is a continuous improvement methodology that focuses on reducing waste. **Six Sigma** is a continuous improvement methodology that focuses on improving the quality of individual processes, and it does so by reducing variation and defects.

Following is a list of tools typically employed in the five steps of DMAIC process improvement. Many of the same tools are employed in both Lean and Six Sigma methodologies.

9

## Typical Six Sigma Tools

1. **D**efine
   - ☐ Flowchart and Value Stream Map
   - ☐ Brainstorming
   - ☐ Pareto Diagram and Analysis
   - ☐ Cause and Effect Diagram and Matrix
   - ☐ SIPOC Diagram (**S**uppliers, **I**nputs, **P**rocess, **O**utputs, **C**ustomers)
   - ☐ QFD Diagram (**Q**uality, **F**unction, Deployment)
   - ☐ Project Charter

2. **M**easure
   - ☐ Data Collection Plan and Sampling
   - ☐ Measurement Techniques and Integrity
   - ☐ Description of Variables
   - ☐ Run Charts and Control Charts
   - ☐ Capabilities Studies

3. **A**nalyze
   - ☐ Gap Analysis and Current State versus Future State
   - ☐ Hypothesis Testing and Confidence Intervals
   - ☐ Analysis of Variance (ANOVA) and Parametric Tests
   - ☐ Correlation and Regression Analysis
   - ☐ Reliability Estimates and Tolerancing Techniques

4. **I**mprove
   - ☐ Implementation Plan
   - ☐ **D**esign of **E**xperiments (DOE)
   - ☐ Pilot Testing
   - ☐ **F**ailure **M**ode **E**ffect **A**nalysis (FMEA)

5. **C**ontrol
   - ☐ Monitoring Plan and Follow-up Actions
   - ☐ **S**tatistical **P**rocess **C**ontrol (SPC)
   - ☐ Dashboard Metrics and Cost-Benefit Analysis
   - ☐ Lessons Learned

9

Many of the tools we have discussed for defining and measuring processes are related to Lean. Six Sigma quality, as the name implies, focuses primarily on statistics and the various tools used for analysis and improvement. These include things such as a description of variables, measurement reliability, statistics important for continuous improvement, hypothesis testing, control charts, process capability analysis, and tools associated with designing experiments for improvement. As a starting point, you need a basic understanding of variables associated with the processes.

## Key Variables Associated with the Process You Want to Improve

The following is a discussion of the basic nature of the key variables associated with the process or processes you want to improve.

***Variables*** are the things you measure, control, or manipulate to improve a process. They differ in many respects, most notably in their inherent nature and in the type of statistical analysis that can be applied.

Variables differ in how well you can measure them. They also differ in how much measurable information their measurement scale can provide. Another factor that determines the information that can be provided by a variable is its type of measurement scale, and variables are classified as nominal, ordinal, interval, or ratio. (Statistics Help. 2015)

> **Nominal variables** allow for only qualitative classification. Typical examples of nominal variables are gender, race, color, and city.
>
> **Ordinal variables** allow rank ordering the items measured in terms of less and more of the quality represented by the variable, but they do not define how much more.
>
> **Interval variables** allow not only rank ordering of the items that are measured, but you can also quantify and compare the differences. For example, temperature, as measured in degrees Fahrenheit or Celsius, constitutes an interval scale.
>
> **Ratio variables** are like interval variables. In addition to all the properties of interval variables, they feature an identifiable absolute zero point. Thus, they allow for statements such as x is two times more than y. Typical examples of ratio scales are measures of time or space.

## Statistics and Continuous Improvement Initiatives

The following discussion describes basic statistics that are used in the analysis phase of a continuous improvement initiative.

9

Remember the bell-shaped curve, which was the statistical method used by some teachers to illustrate test scores and percentages, and to determine who gets what grade?

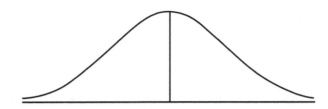

**Normal Distribution (Bell Curve)**

**Statistical methods** are used to compute the mean, mode, median, standard deviation, variance, degree of skew, and kurtosis of variables. Usually, the interest in statistics is with respect to the sample of some population. The larger the sample size, the more reliable the statistics computed from it.

The **mean** or arithmetic average is a particularly informative measure of the average or central tendency of an interval or ratio variable. The **median** is the middle value when a data set is ordered from least to greatest. The **mode** is the number that occurs most often in a data set.

The smaller the variation of data values, the more reliable the mean. Measures of spread concentrate on calculating variation within a data set. The simplest measure of spread is the calculation of the **range** which refers to the difference between the largest and smallest numbers in the data set with the **variance** being the overall difference between the data values and the mean for the data set.

The **standard deviation** and variance are measures of dispersion, that is, the variability of data. Standard deviation is expressed as the following formula:

$$\sigma = \sqrt{\frac{\sum (x\text{-mean})^2}{n}}$$

**σ**  is the symbol used for standard deviation

**Σ**  means sum or addition

**x**  represents a set of numbers. For example, x could be 4, 7, 12, 3, 8

**n**  is the number of values in the data set. For example, for the set above, n = 5

Statistical analysis concepts and tools are not new. The same statistical concepts used in Six Sigma (6σ) continuous improvement methodologies have been used for years. The unique aspect is how they are applied to processes. The chart below illustrates the percentages from 1 to 6 standard deviations from the mean.

**Areas Under the Normal Curve**

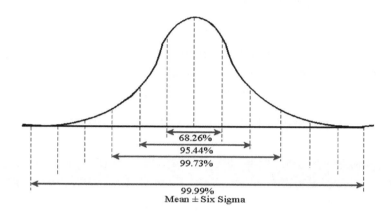

Using the concept of standard deviation and normal distribution, 1σ in each direction of the mean represents 68.26% of the data range, and 6σ represents 99.99% of the data range.

In process improvement efforts a related term or metric is DPMO or defects per million opportunities. Defects in this case refers to any nonconformance to a quality characteristic.

The following table illustrates the DPMO to a Sigma level.

**Six Sigma and Defects per Million**

**Opportunities (DPMO) are quality indices:**

| | | |
|---|---|---|
| 1 Sigma = | 691,463 | DPMO |
| 2 Sigma = | 308,537 | DPMO |
| 3 Sigma = | 66,807 | DPMO |
| 4 Sigma = | 6,210 | DPMO |
| 5 Sigma = | 233 | DPMO |
| **6 Sigma =** | **3.4** | **DPMO** |

9

Advocates of Six Sigma contend the following:

- If you can't express something in numbers, you don't know much about it.
- And if you don't know much about it, you can't control it.
- And if you can't control it, you're at the mercy of chance.

## How good is good enough?

The answer to this question is, well, it depends on how important defect-free or perfection really is **and** at what cost. Is it necessary for your morning coffee to be statistically measured to Six Sigma standards, or must a slice of bread be toasted to perfection? However, for some processes, Six Sigma quality may be crucial.

The following table illustrates what 99 percent versus 99.99966 percent defect-free means:

| 99% Good (3.8 Sigma) | 99.99966% Good (6 Sigma) |
|---|---|
| 20,000 lost articles of mail per hour | 7 articles lost per hour |
| Unsafe drinking water for almost 15 minutes each day | 1 unsafe minute every 7 months |
| 5,000 incorrect surgical operations per week | 1.7 incorrect operations per week |
| 2 short or long landings at most major airports each day | 1 short or long landing every 5 years |
| 200,000 wrong drug prescriptions each year | 68 wrong prescriptions per year |
| No electricity for almost 7 hours each month | 1 hour without electricity every 34 years |

Is flawless execution of each process critical to customer satisfaction? It has been said that in today's business environment, typical work processes are between 3 to 4 sigma. Is 3 to 4 sigma good enough for your work processes, or should you consider designing for improvement?

In our discussions so far, we have focused on the bell-shaped normal curve. However, many distributions are not normally distributed, but skewed one direction or another. The degree of skew is a measure of the *sidedness* of the distribution, that is, the extent to which the distribution of data points is skewed towards the left or right side of the mean.

The **kurtosis** is a measure of *pointedness* or *peakedness* of the distribution, that is, the extent to which the distribution is spread or centered closely around the mean.

Using basic statistical methods, you can construct **frequency distribution** tables, and you can visualize the distributions using charts.

The bell-shaped curves above illustrate **normally distributed data**. Below are examples of **skewed distributions**.

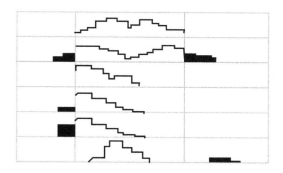

**Examples of Skewed Distributions**

## Statistical Analysis and the Language of Numbers

Data sets can be analyzed and understood using a number of common statistical tools. These include hypothesis testing, reliability studies, process control charts, and the design of experiments. A brief description of these statistical analysis tools follows.

## Test hypotheses (predictions) about your data

You can test hypotheses regarding differences between groups using the ***t*-test** for independent samples, which involves **comparing the means in two groups**. The test assumes that the data in the two groups are normally distributed. If the resultant *t* value is statistically significant, you can conclude that the means in the two groups are different (that is, in the two populations from which the observations were sampled).

Most software results for the ***t*-test** will also include the ***F*-test** for the **comparison of the variances** in the two groups. If statistically significant, you can conclude that the variances (variability) in the two groups are different. The software packages include a probability calculator that allows you to compare a single mean against any hypothesized value.

You can also test for a simple **linear relationship** between two variables by determining the correlation that exists between them. ***Correlation* is a measure of the relation** between two or more variables. The measurement scales used should be at least interval scales, but other correlation coefficients are available to handle other types of data. Correlation coefficients can range from -1.00 to +1.00. The value of -1.00 represents a perfect negative while a value of +1.00 represents a perfect positive correlation. A value of 0.00 represents a lack of correlation.

9

## Evaluate measurement systems for reliability and precision

These statistical procedures typically include those developed for designing and conducting repeatability and reproducibility studies.

*Repeatability* refers to the extent to which repeated measurements of the same item by the same person produce identical results. *Reproducibility* refers to the extent to which different people measuring the same items with the same tools produce identical measurement.

Repeatability and reproducibility can be expressed in terms of variability (across measurements or people, respectively). The size of that variability relative to the variability between items, and the required precision necessary to detect quality problems, determine the reliability, and thus the usefulness of the measurement procedures employed in the quality control effort.

The standard indices of repeatability, reproducibility, and item-to-item variation can be computed, based either on ranges (as is still common in such situations) or by way of analysis of variance methodologies.

## Process Control Charts

The following is a discussion of the ideas behind process control charts and the value of the charts.

In general, process control charts are useful for monitoring an ongoing product or process parameter. In all processes, it is important to monitor the extent to which a product or service meets specifications.

In general terms, there are two **enemies** of product quality: (1) **deviations from target specifications**, and (2) **excessive variability** around target specifications. During the earlier stages of developing the production process, experiments are often designed to optimize these two quality characteristics.

Statistical **process control charts** are sometimes used to monitor the stability and quality of a process as an aid in maintaining statistical control. A process or any operation is said to be in a state of statistical control if, from the evidence gathered from a sample, it can be deduced or inferred with a high degree of confidence that the process or operation is behaving the way it should.

**Statistical Process Control** (SPC) is a tool you can use to determine promptly and inexpensively just when unrealized causes of variation occur, how serious they are, and how they can be prevented from reoccurring.

Below is a simplified process control chart. The **USL** and **LCL** stand for **upper specification limit** and **lower specification limit**. The UCL and LCL stand for upper control limit and lower control limit.

9

**Control Chart**

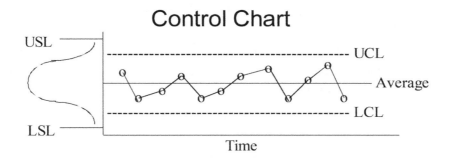

The types of charts are often classified according to the type of quality characteristic they monitor. There are quality control charts for *variables* and control charts for *attributes*. Specifically, the following charts are commonly constructed for controlling variables:

- **X-bar chart**. In this chart the sample *means* are plotted to control the mean value of a variable (such as size, strength, and so on).

- **R chart**. In this chart, the sample *ranges* are plotted to control the variability of a variable.

- **S chart**. In this chart, the sample *standard deviations* are plotted to control the variability of a variable.

## Process Capability

*Process capability* refers to the consistency of a process or the capability of a process to meet its purpose.

All processes have inherent statistical variability that can be evaluated by statistical methods. The range over which the natural variation of a process occurs is determined by the system of **common causes** which include the combination of people, machines, methods, materials, and measurements needed to produce a product or service that will consistently meet design specifications.

Process capability is a measure of the uniformity of the process. It can be measured only if all **special causes** have been eliminated and the process is in a state of statistical control. Capability indices are often used to show the relationship between process capability and process specifications. The two common indices are **Cp** and **Cpk**. Cp measures potential capability and Cpk reflects the current capability. Although the indices are calculated differently, the interpretation is essentially the same.

9

## Analyzing the Gap Between the Current and Future State

Other tools often used for statistical analysis are associated with trying to analyze the gap between the current state and the desired future state of a process. These may include the following:

- **Hypothesis Testing and Confidence Intervals** – Used as a method of making data-driven decisions and determining the level of statistical significance and confidence level.

- **Analysis of Variance (ANOVA) and Parametric Tests** – Used to compare the variances of selected events.

- **Correlation and Regression Analysis** – Used to determine the strength of data relationships.

- **Reliability Estimates and Tolerancing Techniques** – In statistics, reliability typically refers to the consistency of a measure. A measure is said to have high reliability if it produces consistent results under consistent conditions.

You need to be aware of the statistical tools available and their intended use. Software packages are available that explain the tools thoroughly and provide examples of their appropriate use. For most practitioners of Six Sigma methodologies, **Minitab is the most widely used software**. The primary reason is that Minitab collaborated and worked closely with Motorola to meet their needs.

## Design of Experiments and Continuous Improvement

*Design of Experiments* (DOE) has evolved to become a powerful approach to continuous improvement (CI).

As a strategy for planning research, DOE was introduced in the early 1920s when a scientist at an agricultural research station in England, Sir Ronald Fisher, showed how to conduct valid experiments in the presence of many naturally fluctuating conditions such as temperature, soil condition, and rainfall. The design principles that he developed for agricultural experiments have been successfully adapted to industrial and military applications since the 1940s. (Soleimannejed. 2004)

The application of DOE has gained acceptance in the United States as an essential tool for improving the quality of goods and services. This recognition is partially due to the work of Genichi Taguchi, a Japanese quality expert, who promoted the use of DOE in designing *robust products*, which are products relatively insensitive to environmental fluctuations. The recognition is also due to the recent availability of many user-friendly software packages, improved training, and accumulated successes with DOE applications.

9

Designed experiments provide information that helps organizations identify the causes of performance variations and eliminate or reduce such variations by controlling key process parameters, and thereby improve process integrity, service effectiveness, and product quality.

Properly designed and executed experiments generate more precise information while using substantially fewer experimental runs than alternative approaches. They lead to results that can be interpreted using relatively simple statistical techniques, in contrast to the information gathered from archival data, which can be exceedingly difficult to interpret. Simple two-level factorial experimental designs can rapidly increase knowledge about the behavior of the process, service, or product that is the object of improvement.

As previously indicated, statistical software packages such as Minitab provide easy-to-use tools for analyzing data and improving quality, including DOE, and well as all the other tools discussed in this section.

## Failure Mode Effect Analysis (FMEA) / Risk Analysis and Planning Audit (RAPA)

> **"Pay a penny now or a dollar later."**

**Risk** is a significant element of any project, especially large and complex projects, and can be identified during all phases of a project's life cycle. The original scope, cost, and schedule baselines all take risk into account, including the perceived risks categorized by probability and impact.

A **FMEA** is typically used in manufacturing projects as a step-by-step approach for identifying all possible failures in a design or assembly of a product or service. *Failure modes* means the ways, or modes, in which something might fail.

A **RAPA** is typically used in project management for larger projects as an approach to identify all that could potentially go wrong with a project and what actions were – or will be – undertaken to prevent them.

Both the FMEA and RAPA approaches are intended to avoid and mitigate risk. Major reasons for incorporating a formal risk analysis and planning approach include the following:

- Get projects completed on time
- Stay within budget
- Avoid litigation
- Assess safety issues

9

The benefits of a risk analysis and planning approach include the following:

- Reduction of adverse events: reduces stress
- Cost avoidance: reduces the number of project changes
- Versatile: can be applied to almost any improvement project
- Cost effective: adds discipline and structure

## Description of a Failure Mode Effect Analysis (FMEA)

A **FMEA** analysis is typically done by a cross-functional team of subject matter experts. A few types of FMEA analyses exist, such as: functional, design, and process.

The analysis typically occurs early in the product development process and focuses on the product or service design, functionality, and production process. The purpose is to identify risk and correct weaknesses before the product or service gets to the customer.

Numerous variations of FMEA worksheets are available. The following is an example of a FMEA for a Lightweight Glass Bottle (source: Shakehand with Life):

### Failure Mode Effect Analysis (FMEA)

FMEA for Light Weight Glass Bottles

FMEA for Light Weight Glass Bottle

To learn more about how to develop a Failure Mode Effect Analysis, view the video *FMEA Template in Excel to Perform Failure Modes and Effects Analysis* in the Enhance Your Learning section below.

## Description of a Risk Analysis and Planning Audit (RAPA)

The objective of a risk analysis and planning audit is to continue to find potential problems early on, and **not** pass them on.

Guidelines for completing a RAPA are similar to completing a FMEA. Both start with completing a Risk Matrix and Risk Response Plan.

The initial identification of risks should take place in the planning stage of a project. In larger projects, you should consider a risk analysis and planning audit as an ongoing process.

The first step is to clarify what characteristics, requirements, or specifications are important to the organization and the customer, followed by identifying the project requirements that must be met.

Guidelines for completing a project risk analysis and planning audit include completing and updating your **Risk Matrix** and **Risk Response Plan**. Below are definitions for developing and documenting a risk analysis plan.

**Risk Matrix**

| | A. | B. | C. | D. | E. | F. | G. |
|---|---|---|---|---|---|---|---|
| Ref. # | Key Project Activities | Potential Adverse Events | Potential Cause of Adverse Event(s) | Potential Effects of Adverse Event(s) on the Project and Customer | Severity (1-5) | Estimated Impact in Time and Money | Likelihood (1-5) |
| 1 | Resources not available. | | | | | | |
| 2 | | | | | | | |
| n | | | | | | | |

A. **Key Project Activities**. Enter the project activities. Make the descriptions as clear and concise as possible. Be sure to include all activities. If the project stage includes multiple activities and the activities differ greatly, it may be desirable to list the activities separately.

B. **Potential Adverse Event(s)**. An adverse event is a design error or change in the project that prevents it from being completed on time and within budget. Typical adverse events for a simple project might include workers not showing-up, materials delayed, mechanical system problems, and delayed start date. The adverse event is usually expressed in physical terms, not in terms of what the client might experience.

C. **Potential Cause of Adverse Event(s)**. Identify potential causes (root) of the potential adverse event with the objective of potential prevention strategies to minimize the occurrence.

D. **Potential Effects of Adverse Event on the Project and Customer**. The potential effect is what the customer might experience as a result

9

of the adverse event. List all conceivable effects, including violations of government regulations. Group together any effects that are similar or have equal severity.

E. **Severity**. A subjective estimate or judgment of how severe the customer will perceive the effect of the adverse event or how it might impact the project. For discussion purposes, the scale of 1 to 5, shown below, will be used:

| Rating | Severity or Impact Criteria |
|--------|------------------------------|
| 1 | **Negligible severity.** It is unreasonable to think that this effect would impact the project's completion. The client will probably not notice the adverse event. |
| 2 | **Mild severity.** The effect would cause only a slight annoyance. The client will not notice any project performance change. Correction can be done before completion of project. |
| 3 | **Moderate severity.** The client will notice and tolerate adverse event. Correction is inexpensive with little project delay. |
| 4 | **High severity.** The client will notice an intolerable effect. Delays are expensive. Areas possibly subject to government regulations or safety hazards. |
| 5 | **Very high severity.** Dangerous effect may occur without warning. Nonconformance to laws. |

F. **Estimated Impact in Time and Money**. An estimate of the impact in terms of the magnitude of time or money associated with the potential adverse effect.

G. **Likelihood**. A subjective estimate or judgment of the probability that the cause and, therefore, the adverse event will occur. For discussion purposes, the scale of 1 to 5, shown below, will be used:

| Rating | Likelihood or Probability Criteria |
|--------|-------------------------------------|
| 1 | It is highly unlikely that an adverse event will occur. |
| 2 | The adverse event would occur only under rare circumstances. |
| 3 | Adverse event is somewhat likely. |
| 4 | Adverse event is very likely. |
| 5 | Almost certain that an adverse event will occur. |

9

## Risk Response Plan

| Ref. # | Recommended Actions to Eliminate or Enhance Prevention or Detection | Effectiveness (1-5) | Risk Priority Number (RPN) | Responsibility for Action Accepted by | What Actions Can You Take If It Does Occur? | Action Priority (A-E) |
|--------|-----|-----|-----|-----|-----|-----|
| 1 | Authorize Overtime | | | | | |

H. **Recommended Actions to Eliminate or Enhance Prevention or Detection**. Enter recommended actions for reducing the severity and likelihood that an adverse event will occur, or for improving the effectiveness of the prevention or detection methods.

I. **Effectiveness**. A subjective estimate or judgment of how effectively the prevention or detection measure eliminates potential adverse events. It quantifies judgment of the soundness of a design feature or inspection procedure, the validity of a test, the sufficiency of a final test, and so on. For discussion purposes, the scale of 1 to 5, shown below, will be used:

| Rating | Effectiveness Criteria |
|--------|-----|
| 1 | The prevention or detection measure is foolproof. There is no chance that the adverse event might still occur. |
| 2 | The likelihood of the adverse event occurring is low. |
| 3 | Moderate likelihood. The prevention or detection method is effective only sometimes; the cause occurs repeatedly. |
| 4 | High likelihood. The prevention or detection method is effective only sometime; the adverse event occurs repeatedly. |
| 5 | Very high likelihood. The prevention or detection measure is ineffective. The adverse event will occur. |

J. **Risk Priority Number**: The Risk Priority Number (RPN) is the product of the severity, likelihood, and effectiveness ratings. For example:

| Severity | | Likelihood | | Effectiveness | | RPN |
|----------|---|------------|---|---------------|---|-----|
| 4 | x | 5 | x | 3 | = | 60 |

Every adverse event has an RPN. Through rank ordering the RPNs you can determine what adverse event is most critical and assign it priority for corrective action.

9

K. **Responsibility for action accepted by**. Enter the name of the individual on the project team who has the authority to implement the corrective action.

L. **What Actions Can You Take If It Does Occur?** Identify what specific actions you can take if the event does occur.

M. **Action Priority**. Assign priorities to the recommended corrective action by considering the RPN and other factors. High priority should always be given to corrective actions associated without adverse event of high severity. Below, for discussion purposes, is one method of classification:

| R.P.N. | Priority Classification | Description |
|---|---|---|
| 100-125 | A | Action must be taken or implemented before project begins or immediately. |
| 75-99 | B | Action must be initiated or resolved or implemented within a week. |
| 50-74 | C | Action must be initiated or resolved or implemented within a month. |
| 25-49 | D | Action may or may not be pursued. |
| 1-24 | E | Action will not be pursued. |

Adverse events may occur at anytime throughout the lifecycle of a project. A risk analysis and planning audit (RAPA) is performed to assure that all that could potentially go wrong with a project has been recognized and that actions were or will be taken to prevent them.

A sample Risk Analysis and Planning Audit (RAPA) Worksheet is available in Appendix J.

## Work Processes Where Six Sigma Methodologies Can Be Useful

In some work processes, such as making toast, Six Sigma may be considered overkill and unwarranted. However, for critical work processes where the potential benefits outweigh the costs of conducting the analysis, such methodologies should be considered.

Typical work processes where Six Sigma may be useful include the following:

- Making a critical product or product component
- Billing and invoicing customers
- Lending money
- Servicing engines or specific pieces of equipment
- Tracking medical prescriptions and records

---

### Process Improvement Case Study: Mitigate Product Failures

**Current State**: A large multi-national manufacturing organization experienced unexplained failures in one of their core products. This caused millions of dollars in lawsuits, and product failures were also alleged to have contributed to many deaths. A Failure Mode Effect Analysis (FMEA) had been initially performed during the product design stage to identify risks. However, a variety of unexplained failures persisted resulting in the loss of life and substantial legal claims. As a result, a series of experiments were designed to test several hypotheses.

**Future State**: Data was analyzed to determine the root cause(s) and make corrections. Six Sigma tools were applied to analyze the situation. The analysis pointed to, among other things, a lack of material specification knowledge and inadequate training. Simply put, the designers "didn't know what they didn't know." They lacked the knowledge and experience to properly specify the materials used, which resulted in the unexpected and tragic failures.

**Impact**: FMEA and EOE analysis proved to be invaluable tools in helping to identify and mitigate future disastrous outcomes. Material specifications were revised and communicated. New qualifications and training for designers were required.

---

## WHAT TO DO:

☐ Understand that the DMAIC process (**D**efine, **M**easure, **A**nalyze, **I**mprove, and **C**ontrol) is synonymous with the process for achieving Six Sigma quality.

☐ Know that the two enemies of quality are deviations from target specifications and excessive variability.

☐ Identify the Six Sigma tools appropriate for planning and perfecting the future state of your process.

9

Other actions:

☐ _____

☐ _____

☐ _____

**Remember**

✓ Six Sigma is a statistical measurement (6 σ); meaning six standard deviations between the process mean and the nearest specification limit.

✓ Six Sigma is also a business philosophy, strategy, methodology, and threshold of excellence initially developed by Motorola in the 1970s.

**Enhance Your Learning**

Watch the 14-minute review of Concept 9:

***Six-Sigma Quality*** (2016)

(click on the image to launch video)

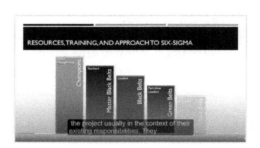

Watch the three-minute video for an overview of the use and value of developing a FMEA using Excel:

***FMEA Template in Excel to Perform Failure Modes and Effects Analysis*** (2010)

9

For a good summary of Six Sigma watch the following 9-minute video:

***Six Sigma In 9 Minutes | Simplilearn*** (2020)

For a fun three-minute video about six sigma from "That 70's Show" at:

***What is Six Sigma? - FUN VERSION*** (2011)

This four-minute video gives an introduction on how Six Sigma can affect any business:

***What Six Sigma Can Do For Your Business?*** (2014)

To learn more about elementary concepts in statistics watch this 12-minute video:

***Statistics: The average | Descriptive statistics | Probability and Statistics | Khan Academy*** (2009)

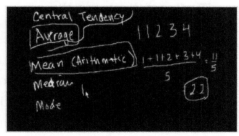

Review the following website for a set of tools for applying both Lean and Six Sigma:

***The MoreSteam Toolbox*** (2020)

9

**Reinforce Your Learning**

**Six Sigma Tools Checklist**. For the process you identified as the focus for applying Lean Sigma tools and methodologies, check what Six Sigma tools may be appropriate to use for your process improvement project.

1. **D**efine
   - ☐ Flowchart and Value Stream Map
   - ☐ Brainstorming
   - ☐ Pareto Diagram and Analysis
   - ☐ Cause and Effect Diagram and Matrix
   - ☐ SIPOC Diagram (Suppliers, Inputs, Process, Outputs, Customers)
   - ☐ QFD Diagram (Quality, Function, Deployment)
   - ☐ Project Charter

2. **M**easure
   - ☐ Data Collection Plan and Sampling
   - ☐ Measurement Techniques and Integrity
   - ☐ Description of Variables
   - ☐ Run Charts and Control Charts
   - ☐ Capabilities Studies

3. **A**nalyze
   - ☐ Gap Analysis and Current State versus Future State
   - ☐ Hypothesis Testing and Confidence Intervals
   - ☐ Analysis of Variance (ANOVA) and Parametric Tests
   - ☐ Correlation and Regression Analysis
   - ☐ Reliability Estimates and Tolerancing Techniques

4. **I**mprove
   - ☐ Implementation Plan
   - ☐ Design of Experiments (DOE)
   - ☐ Pilot Testing
   - ☐ Failure Mode Effect Analysis (FMEA)

5. **C**ontrol
   - ☐ Monitoring Plan and Follow-up Actions
   - ☐ Statistical Process Control (SPC)
   - ☐ Dashboard Metrics and Cost-Benefit Analysis
   - ☐ Lessons Learned

9

# Prepare Initiative Justifications and Reports

Naturally, no one size fits all. The content and presentation style for reporting the results of a typical Lean Six Sigma project will depend on your audience and purpose.

If your stakeholders are familiar with your improvement project, an informal discussion may be all that is needed for reporting results and to proceed with implementation. However, if you work in an environment with bureaucracy, politics, or a multitude of stakeholders with diverse levels of knowledge, more formal reporting methods and documentation may be warranted.

No matter how you report your project, you should include an analysis of the costs and benefits associated with the project recommendations. A cost-benefit analysis identifies the costs associated with a process versus the benefits of taking an action. There is no one way to do a cost-benefit analysis. All the concepts discussed here can go into the analysis.

## Cost-Benefit Analysis and Project Justifications

Business and project leaders must choose among project alternatives. Alternatives can be evaluated and ranked in terms of costs and benefits. This means doing a cost-benefit analysis and comparing different potential products, services, or project initiatives.

An analysis like this can be a type of quantitative input to the decision-making process. Of course, costs are not the only way to decide among alternatives. Use your experience and obtain qualitative input from other knowledgeable people as you weigh your options. Justifications for a recommended action may include quantifiable and non-quantifiable elements.

**Quantifiable** elements are things such as anticipated profit, the future value of money, and a competitive analysis. **Non-quantifiable elements** (qualitative) might include your experience, your gut feeling for turns in the marketplace, consumer surveys, and other factors such as safety and regulatory compliance.

10

However, one important consideration in decision making is typically calculating the **return on investment** (ROI) and **payback** of project initiatives. This helps you decide among projects competing for limited resources such as money.

Organizations compare project initiatives in various ways. However, most include ROI and payback as required components in their decision-making process.

You can *calculate ROI* using the following formula:

> **Return On Investment = (Benefit – Cost) / Cost**

*Or, as a percentage*

> **ROI = [(Project's Financial Benefit – Project's Cost) / Project Cost] x 100%**

Also look at the *payback period*, which is how long a new project or initiative will take to be profitable. For example, installing solar panels on your roof might save you money on energy bills in the long run, but they might cost tens of thousands of dollars today. Consider how long it would take to pay for the panels when deciding if the expenditure is worth it.

> **Payback Period = (Project Investment / Annual Cash Flow) x 12 Months**

As an example of ROI and payback, assume a process improvement project would cost $22,000 to implement and that it has a useful life of three years. This initiative would result in a five percent increase in output and net income of an operation that generates $300,000 in net income per year.

Using the formulas above, this investment would translate to a Benefit of $45,000 and ROI of 104%

Benefit = $300,000 x 0.05 = $15,000 per year x 3 years = $45,000

ROI = (($45,000 - $22,000) /$22,000) x 100% = 104%

The payback period reported in months would be 17.6 months.

Payback Period = ($22,000/ $15,000) x 12 months = 17.6 months

## Presenting Project Initiatives

In most work environments, the following outline for presenting typical Lean Six Sigma projects should be sufficient. You can modify the tools you use and your report format to fit your project. However, it is advisable to share the spotlight with everyone who contributed to the project.

10

Busy professionals who have many responsibilities can sometimes have a short attention span. For the type of projects discussed here, a 10 to 20-minute informal presentation to present the findings and recommendations to the decision makers, followed by a discussion period of 5 to 10 minutes, would be appropriate. A formal report may also be useful, one that summarizes the essential data, the analysis, and the findings.

If a formal presentation to a broader audience is warranted, a professional looking PowerPoint presentation may be appropriate.

If a PowerPoint presentation is appropriate, consider using assertion-based slides and techniques to convey your message. Assertion-based slides typically start with a sentence headline that states the primary assertion of the slide. That headline assertion is then supported not by a bullet list, but by visual evidence such as photos, drawings, diagrams, graphs, and embedded video.

The contents of a typical Lean Six Sigma presentation should cover the relevant tools employed. For most projects, a report and presentation might include the following basic tools:

- Value Stream Map
- SIPOC Diagram
- Cause and Effect (Fishbone) Diagram
- 5 Whys
- Spaghetti Diagram
- 5S Assessment
- A3 Problem Solving Worksheet (Current State and Future State)
- Documentation of observations, data, and analysis, including a Return on Investment study (ROI=Cost/Benefit)
- Lessons Learned

However, some Lean Six Sigma projects may be more complex and incorporate statistical analysis elements.  if your project is more involved and warrants the use of statistical analysis elements, you should consider selecting additional tools from the following expanded Lean Sigma Tools Checklist that follows. A blank Lean Six Sigma Tools Checklist is available in Appendix K.

10

## Lean Six Sigma Tools Checklist

### Current State and Situation Analysis

☐ Project Scope or Charter Statement

☐ Flowchart or Process Map

☐ Value Stream Map (Current State)

☐ Data Collection Plan and Sampling (data reported in Value Stream Map)

☐ Observation Data Worksheets and Charts

☐ SIPOC Diagram (Suppliers, Inputs, Process, Outputs, Customers)

☐ Structured Brainstorming

☐ Cause and Effect Diagram and Matrix

☐ Pareto Diagram and Analysis (most important issues from customer's perspective)

☐ Run Charts and Control Charts

☐ Capabilities Studies

☐ QFD Diagram (Quality, Function, Deployment)

☐ Root Cause Analysis (5 Whys)

☐ Hypothesis Testing and Confidence Intervals

☐ Analysis of Variance (ANOVA) and Parametric Tests

☐ Correlation and Regression Analysis

☐ Reliability Estimates and Tolerancing Techniques

### Future State and Implementation

☐ A3 Problem Solving Worksheet and Gap Analysis

☐ Spaghetti Charts

☐ Cellular – Modular Flow Diagram

☐ Workplace Organization and 5S Tools (Sort, Straighten, Scrub, Standardize, Sustain)

☐ Just in Time (JIT)

☐ Quick Changeover and Set-Up Reduction

☐ Pull and Kanban (Visible Record)

☐ Countermeasures and Poka-Yoke (mistake proofing)

☐ Visual Management

☐ Total Productive Maintenance (TPM)

☐ Design of Experiments (DOE)

10

- ☐ Failure Mode Effect Analysis (FMEA)
- ☐ Risk Analysis and Planning Audit (RAPA)
- ☐ Implementation Plan (Who, What, Where, When, Why, How)
- ☐ Pilot Testing
- ☐ Dashboard Metrics and Cost-Benefit Analysis
- ☐ Monitoring Plan and Follow-up Actions
- ☐ Lessons Learned

---

## Process Improvement Case Study: Risk and Reward

**Current State**: Customers are reluctant to try new, risky technologies, but that might be the only option if their demanding requirements are to be met. When products fail in qualification testing, it is frustrating for everyone because time and costs start to add up beyond what anyone wants.

**Future State**: Pursue robust Failure Mode and Effects Analysis (FMEA) and more structured brainstorming efforts. Initiate a systematic process of going through each element of the design and its interactions between parts and environment and include the customer. Such efforts often include designing appropriate experiments.

**Impact**: Catch mistakes and errors before they become problems. A Design of Experiments (DOE) analysis aims to describe and explain the variation of information under conditions that are hypothesized to reflect the variation. An FMEA would force individuals to rank and prioritize failure modes and causes so that variables and potential actions can be vetted, tested, and justified. The FMEA also serves as a mechanism to educate responsible individuals about inherent risks, probability of occurrence, and planned mitigation efforts.

---

## WHAT TO DO:

- ☐ Prepare a cost-benefit analysis to justify your proposed improvement initiative.
- ☐ Recognize that both quantifiable and qualitative elements should be considered when choosing among alternative investment options.
- ☐ Prepare a 10 to 20-minute presentation, and incorporate the appropriate Lean tools and lessons learned.

10

Other actions:

☐ _____

☐ _____

☐ _____

- ✓ A picture is worth a thousand words, which is another way of saying you are advised to show and not just tell. Try using assertion-based based PowerPoint slides. Assertion slides typically start with a sentence headline that states the main assertion of the slide. That headline assertion is then supported not by a bullet list, but by visual evidence such as photos, drawings, diagrams, graphs, and embedded video clips.

- ✓ You have earned the right to talk, but do not try to give a speech. Plan the main points that convey the message you want to deliver. Your message should focus on the goal of Lean to eliminate waste and variation in work systems and processes.

- ✓ Busy professionals may have a short attention span. For the type of projects discussed in this guide, a 10-minute presentation to present the findings and recommendations followed by a discussion period of 5 to 10 minutes is appropriate.

10

**Enhance Your Learning**

Watch the six-minute review: Preparing for Project Initiative Report-Outs:

***Preparing for Project Initiative Report-Outs*** (2016)

(click on the image to launch video)

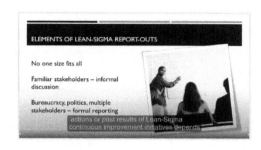

Watch the nine-minute video for an overview of the Design of Experiments (DOE) process:

***Learn How Powerful a Design of Experiment (DOE) Can Be When Leveraged Correctly*** (2013)

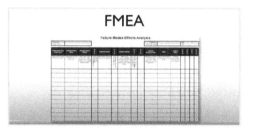

Watch the seven-minute video to learn more about calculate Return On Investment:

***Return On Investment ("ROI")*** (2019)

Review the following website that provides a set of tools for giving effective technical presentations using assertion-evidence slides:

***Rethinking Scientific Presentations: The Assertion-Evidence Approach*** (2020)

10

Watch the five-minute video on how Steven Jobs prepared for giving presentations:

***5 Tips for Giving a Presentation the Steve Jobs Way*** (2009)

 **Reinforce Your Learning**

**Your Report Presentation**. For the process you identified as the focus for applying Lean tools and methodologies, prepare a 10 to 20-minute presentation that incorporates and demonstrates the use of the following typical basic Lean Six Sigma tools and others that are relevant to your process. Use assertion-based PowerPoint slides. The organization and flow of the presentation should follow the format of the A3 Problem Solving process (Issue, Background, Current State, Situation Analysis, and so on).

- Value Stream Map
- SIPOC Diagram
- Cause and Effect (Fishbone) Diagram
- 5 Whys
- Spaghetti Diagram
- 5S Assessment
- A3 Problem Solving Worksheet (Current State and Future State)
- Documentation of observations, data, and analysis, including a Return on Investment study (ROI=Cost Benefit)
- Lessons Learned

Present your project initiative to interested stakeholders. Distribute a copy of the presentation, either digitally or in hard copy.

Note: if your project is more involved and warrants the use of statistical analysis elements, you should consider selecting additional tools from the expanded Lean Sigma Tools Checklist. A blank Lean Six Sigma Tools Checklist is available in Appendix K.

10

# A Final Word:
## *Applying Lean Six Sigma*

The purpose of this guide is to give you a better understanding of Lean Six Sigma tools and how you can apply them to continuous improvement initiatives and projects in your organization. The guide focuses on the roles these tools play in helping you achieve organizational success.

In this guide you learned about:

- Lean Six Sigma and how these principles, best practices, and tools fit with other continuous improvement methodologies.

- How you can use Lean Six Sigma to improve your work processes.

- Approaches for applying Lean Six Sigma concepts to practical applications.

- A3 Problem Solving methodology, including current state and future state analysis.

- Typical cross-industry project reporting and presentation formats.

Take a few minutes to reflect on how you might apply what you learned in the guide and how you have expanded your skills and knowledge relevant to Lean Six Sigma.

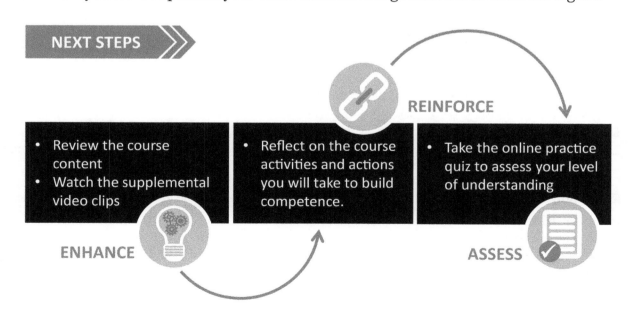

# Unlocking Lean Six Sigma Recap Checklist

While Lean Six Sigma concepts have their roots in manufacturing, studies show that people have achieved similar results in financial services, healthcare, and government. The focus of Lean Six Sigma as a continuous improvement methodology and process management strategy is to improve processes and eliminate waste.

1. **Differentiate Lean and Six Sigma Methodologies**
   - ☐ Describe the differences and commonalities between Lean and Six Sigma methodologies.
   - ☐ Think about products you rely on in daily life and how they have changed over the past decade.
   - ☐ Identify one product or service that frustrates you and that needs improvement.

2. **Describe Lean and Categories of Waste**
   - ☐ Be mindful that customers pay only for what is of use to them and gives them value.
   - ☐ Recognize that at least 85 percent of problems (and waste) are in systems.
   - ☐ Identify one work process you believe warrants further examination for improvement.

3. **Observe Processes and Scope Improvement Initiatives**
   - ☐ Observe a work process and document your findings using an Observation Worksheet.
   - ☐ Decide who else should participate in possible improvement efforts.
   - ☐ Complete a Lean Six Sigma Project Scope Statement for your work process.

4. **Diagram Using Flowcharts and Process Maps**
   - ☐ Develop a high-level (five to seven steps) flowchart of your problematic work process.
   - ☐ Assemble stakeholders and brainstorm the inputs, outputs, suppliers, and customers of your process.
   - ☐ Complete a SIPOC diagram for your process.

5. **Collect Data on Value Streams**
   - ☐ Document how an improvement request will be communicated in the top part of the VSM.
   - ☐ Insert your flowchart or process map with appropriate symbols in the middle part of the VSM.
   - ☐ Insert metrics using a Saw-tooth diagram in the lower part of the VSM.

6. **Understand the A3 Problem Solving Methodology**
   - ☐ Focus on the part of a process that will yield the most significant benefits.
   - ☐ Identify tools that may be useful and that will help you analyze the root causes of process problems.
   - ☐ Determine what tools you can apply to your improvement initiative.

7. **Apply Tools for Analyzing the Current Situation**
   - ☐ Brainstorm the barriers and challenges of the current process.
   - ☐ Categorize and consolidate the ideas generated using the four primary categories (people, methods, materials, and machines), or other categories as appropriate.
   - ☐ Input the categorized ideas into a Cause and Effect diagram.

8. **Apply Tools for Future State Planning**
   - ☐ Sketch the desired future state of your problematic process.
   - ☐ Determine how you will implement the 5S methodology to improve and sustain planned actions.
   - ☐ Develop a Standard Work Plan by outlining the steps and timing of your future state.

9. **Identify Tools for Six Sigma Quality**
   - ☐ Understand that the DMAIC process (Define, Measure, Analyze, Improve, and Control) is synonymous with the process for achieving Six Sigma quality.
   - ☐ Know that the two enemies of quality are deviations from specifications and excessive variability.
   - ☐ Identify the Six Sigma tools appropriate for planning and perfecting the future state of your process.

10. **Prepare Initiative Justifications and Report**
    - ☐ Prepare a cost-benefit analysis to justify your proposed improvement initiative.
    - ☐ Recognize that both quantifiable and qualitative elements should be considered when choosing among alternative investment options.
    - ☐ Report your findings in a 10 to 20-minute presentation, and incorporate the appropriate Lean Six Sigma tools and lessons learned.

*The most dangerous kind of waste is the waste we don't recognize.*

– Shigeo Shingo

# Sources and Citations

Alley, M. (2020). *Rethinking Scientific Presentations: The Assertion-Evidence Approach*. Retrieved from: https://www.youtube.com/watch?v=795oIuJoRHg

Alley, M. (2003). *The Craft of Scientific Presentations: Critical Steps to Succeed and Critical Errors to Avoid.*

ASQ website (2020). Retrieved at: http://asq.org/index.aspx

Baldridge Performance Excellence Program. (2020). http://www.nist.gov/baldrige/

Baldwin, C. (2020). *Introduction to Process Flow Charts (Lean Six Sigma)*. Retrieved from: https://www.youtube.com/watch?v=wLkvvqypq1E

Ballal, A. (2020). *Brainstorming | Structured brainstorming*. Retrieved from: https://www.youtube.com/watch?v=5VBodEnZzzQ

Berman, A. (2017). *Just in Time by Toyota: The Smartest Production System in The World*. Retrieved from: https://www.youtube.com/watch?v=cAUXHJBB5CM

ClayTrader. (2019). *Return On Investment ("ROI")*. Retrieved from: https://www.youtube.com/watch?v=LCiHGuTIuLk

Crosby, P. (Classic 1979). *Quality is Free.*

Denver Public Health. (2016). *A3 Problem Solving Tool*. Retrieved from: https://www.youtube.com/watch?v=JaVMUoQBygE

Elsevier, Inc. (2016). *Impact of lean six sigma process improvement methodology on cardiac catheterization laboratory efficiency*. US National Library of Medicine, National Center for Biotechnical Information. Retrieved from: https://www.ncbi.nlm.nih.gov/pubmed/26905051

EPM. (2020). *Fishbone Diagram Explained with Example*. Retrieved from: https://www.youtube.com/watch?v=JbRx5pw-efg&t=98s

Four Principles. (2013). *Four Principles TPM*. Retrieved from: https://www.youtube.com/watch?v=nb031_LQIHQ

Gallo, C. (2009). *5 Tips for Giving a Presentation the Steve Jobs Way*. Retrieved from: https://www.youtube.com/watch?v=2tBn4tOmIVY

GBMP. (2017). *GBMP Lean Training DVD: Toast Kaizen - Introduction to Lean Manufacturing Preview.* Retrieved from: https://www.youtube.com/watch?v=3N89JJ991pE

Gemba Academy (2019). *Gemba Walk: Where the Real Work Happens.* Retrieved from: https://www.youtube.com/watch?v=-2hSveoJbxc

Gemba Academy. (2013). *Learn How Powerful a Design of Experiment (DOE) Can Be When Leveraged Correctly.* Retrieved from: https://www.youtube.com/watch?v=tZWAYbKYVjM

George, M., Rowlands, D., Kastle, B. (2004). *What is Lean Six Sigma?*

George, M., Rowlands, D., Price, M., Maxey, J. (2005). *Lean Six Sigma Toolbook.*

Girdler, A. (2019). *SIPOC Diagram Simplified [SIPOC Tutorial].* Retrieved from: https://www.youtube.com/watch?v=9MRDoroDQB4

Girdler, A. (2020). *How to Value Stream Map [STEP BY STEP].* Retrieved from: https://www.youtube.com/watch?v=7wD7R6x3Pv4

Gupta, P. (2004). *Six Sigma Business Scorecard.*

Haris, H. (2010). *QFD For Pizza.* Retrieved from: https://www.slideshare.net/MuhammadHaris/qrd-for-pizza

Harry, M. (1988). *The Nature of Six Sigma Quality.*

Hauser. J., and Clausing, D. (2016). *The House of Quality.* Harvard Business Review. Retrieved from: https://hbr.org/1988/05/the-house-of-quality

Hunter, D. (2013). *The History of Lean Thinking.* Retrieved from: https://www.youtube.com/watch?v=v2KN8CCfu_E

Khan Academy. (2009). *Statistics: The average | Descriptive statistics | Probability and Statistics | Khan Academy.* Retrieved from: https://www.youtube.com/watch?v=uhxtUt_-GyM&list=PL1328115D3D8A2566

Lean Consulting Ltd. (2015). *Lean Tools - Value Stream Mapping.* Retrieved from: https://www.youtube.com/watch?v=vbnLl285gyY

Lean Enterprise Institute. (2018). *The 5 Whys - Lean Problem Solving.* Retrieved from: https://www.youtube.com/watch?v=SrlYkx41wEE

Lean Smarts. (2019). *Introduction to 5S Methodology Training - Lean Manufacturing Principles*. Retrieved from: https://www.youtube.com/watch?v=SODLdxMkVAM

Liker, J. (2004). *The Toyota Way.*

MacInnes, R. L. (2009). *The lean enterprise memory jogger for service*. Salem, NH: GOAL QPC.

Moresteam. (2020). *Process Improvement & Lean Six Sigma Toolbox*. Retrieved from: https://www.moresteam.com/toolbox/

OpsExcellence. (2015). *Takt Time, Cycle Time, Lead Time.* https://www.youtube.com/watch?v=isu6MG3v0-s

Osborn, A.F. (Classic. 1963) *Applied imagination: Principles of Creative Problem Solving.*

Pande, P., Neuman, R., Cavanagh, R. (2002). *The Six Sigma Way – Team Fieldbook.*

OIMacros. (2010). *Toyota A3 Report Template in Excel*. Retrieved from: https://www.youtube.com/watch?v=6WvwR_IU3-8

QIMacros. (2010). *FMEA Template in Excel to Perform Failure Modes and Effects Analysis*. Retrieved from: https://www.youtube.com/watch?v=TxD3gTd6jnE

Quantum Lean. (2019). *Lean manufacturing standard work made simple*. Retrieved from: https://www.youtube.com/watch?v=k4zwOO2mya8

Schroeder, R. Harry, M. (2006). *Six Sigma: The Breakthrough Management Strategy Revolutionizing the World's Top Corporations.*

Schuster Engineering. (2019). *Quality Function Deployment (QFD) Example*. Retrieved from: https://www.youtube.com/watch?v=m2n0W1ycolY

Simplilearn. (2020). *Six Sigma In 9 Minutes | What Is Six Sigma? | Six Sigma Explained | Six Sigma Training | Simplilearn*. Retrieved from: https://www.youtube.com/watch?v=4EDYfSl-fmc

Six Sigma Academy Amsterdam. (2019). *Quality Function Deployment (QFD) House of Quality*. Retrieved from: https://www.youtube.com/watch?v=6vfXX_njzvE

Six Sigma Daily. (2014). *What Six Sigma Can Do For Your Business - What is Six Sigma?* Retrieved from: https://www.youtube.com/watch?v=oSYrjCCECD4

Six Sigma Organization. (2012). *A3 Problem Solving*. Retrieved from: https://www.youtube.com/watch?v=ZR2qZd4mVwA

Sobek, D. (2001). *A3 Process*. National Science Foundation.

Soleimannejed, F. (2004). *Six Sigma, Basic Steps & Implementation*. AuthorHouse

Spear, S., Bowen, H. (2006). *Decoding the DNA of the Toyota Production System*.

Statistics Help. (2015). *Elementary Concepts in Statistics*. Retrieved from: http://documentation.statsoft.com/STATISTICAHelp.aspx?path=Statistics/ElementaryConcepts/ElementaryConcepts

The Lean Six Sigma Company. (2014). *What is Lean Six Sigma? The power of combining the two methods*. Retrieved from: https://www.youtube.com/watch?v=PHOppLiEG0o

Vector Solutions. (2020). *Lean Manufacturing - Standardized Work*. https://www.youtube.com/watch?v=TxK9lYS6jKM

Virtual Kaizen Coach. (2020). *What is the Difference Between Lean and Six Sigma*. Retrieved from: https://www.youtube.com/watch?v=76iJK2OEcWk

WhatissixsigmaNET. (2011). *What is Six Sigma? - FUN VERSION*. Retrieved from: https://www.youtube.com/watch?v=H4vZN-cMJyY

Wedgwood, I. (2007). *Lean Sigma – A Practitioner's Guide*.

Womack, J., Jones, D., Roos, D. (1990). *The Machine That Changed the World*.

Womack, J., Jones, D. (2003). *Lean Thinking*.

Wujec, T. (2013). *Got a wicked problem? First, tell me how you make toast*. Retrieved from: https://www.ted.com/talks/tom_wujec_got_a_wicked_problem_first_tell_me_how_you_make_toast

U.S. Federal Highway Administration. (2001). *Continuous Process Improvement: Tools and Techniques for Practitioners*.

# Earn PDHs and a Lean Sigma Yellow Belt Credential

Centrestar provides online short courses where you have the option of earning professional development hours (PDHs) and a Centrestar Lean Sigma Process Improvement Yellow Belt.

To earn 12 PDHs and the Yellow Belt credential, you can study the content of this guide at home or work, complete the Centrestar Knowledge Review – Practice Test that follows, then compare your answers with the correct answers which are at the end of the test.

When ready to take the actual test, register for the Lean Sigma Process Improvement Yellow Belt course (CPE 1204) at www.centrestar.com

After you register, submit the payment fee noted, and login, you can review the same content materials or simply go straight to the Knowledge Review section and take the Test.

Successful completion requires a passing score of 80%. Upon completion, download your Lean Sigma Process Improvement Yellow Belt certificate.

*Practice isn't the thing you do once you're good.*
*It's the thing you do that makes you good.*

– Malcolm Gladwell

# Lean Six Sigma Knowledge Review - Practice Test

(CPE 1204: 120 questions total)

## Concept 1 – Differentiate Lean and Six Sigma Methodologies

1. Which of the following is NOT a potential benefit that organizations experience from implementing Lean initiatives?

    A. Improved cash flow

    B. Reduced inventory

    C. Improved quality

    D. Reduced waste

    E. All the above are potential benefits of Lean initiatives

2. Six Sigma is a continuous improvement methodology originally developed and trademarked by:

    A. Penn State

    B. General Electric

    C. The Brookings Institute

    D. Motorola

    E. Toyota

3. Lean is a production practice that considers the expenditure of resources for any goal other than the creation of value for the end customer to be wasteful, and thus a target for elimination. What organization first implemented the methodology?

    A. Massachusetts Institute Technology (MIT)

    B. Toyota

    C. Weight Watchers

    D. Motorola

    E. Perdue Agribusiness

4. The primary focus of Six Sigma methodology is improving the quality of products and processes by reducing:

    A. Waste

    B. Variation and defects

    C. Weight

    D. Temperature

   E.  None of the above

5.   Six Sigma methodology follows a top-down strategy and Lean follows a bottoms-up strategy.

   A.  True
   B.  False

6.   The term Sigma in the mathematical context refers to:

   A.  Standard deviation or variance from the mean average
   B.  99.9%
   C.  Absolute zero
   D.  Positive integers equaling 1.0
   E.  Infinity

7.   Total Quality Management (TQM) is an inclusive philosophy that incorporates many of the tools common to Lean, Six Sigma and project management for continuously improving the quality of products and processes. TQM was a term coined by many American management consultants, including:

   A.  W. Edwards Deming
   B.  Joseph Juran
   C.  Phil Crosby
   D.  All the above
   E.  None of the above

8.   Project management is the discipline of planning, organizing, and managing resources to bring about the successful completion of a specific project. The project management cycle typically includes the following elements:

   A.  Define, measure, analyze, improve, control
   B.  Observe, map, problem solve, optimization
   C.  Initiation, planning, evaluation, controlling, and closing
   D.  Clarify goal, define options, gather facts, implement, follow-up
   E.  Plan, do, check, act

9.   Both Lean and Six Sigma advocate a focus on leadership and on improving performance results as evidenced by the Baldrige Framework for Performance Excellence and its emphasis on both Lean and Six Sigma.

   A.  True
   B.  False

10. The Baldrige Criteria for Performance Excellence is administered by which of these groups?

    A. The Employment and Training Administration, an agency of the U.S. Department of Labor

    B. The Occupational Safety and Health Administration (OSHA), an agency of the U.S. Department of Labor

    C. The National Institute of Standards and Technology, an agency of the U.S. Department of Commerce

    D. The U.S. Office of Management and Budget (OMB)

    E. The U. S. Office of Personnel Management (OPM)

    **Answer**: C. National Institute of Standards and Technology, an agency of the U.S. Department of Commerce.

11. While both Lean Sigma and Six Sigma had their roots in manufacturing, Lean Sigma methodologies can be applied best in:

    A. Service organizations

    B. Healthcare

    C. Government

    D. Low-tech or high-tech operations

    E. Any organization whose leadership is committed to continuous improvement

12. The purpose of organizations pursuing Lean initiatives is to:

    A. Obtain awards

    B. Stay competitive

    C. Positive public relations

    D. Appease the shareholders

    E. Meet government regulations

## Concept 2 – Describe Lean and Categories of Waste

13. By definition, the traditional focus of Lean is to systematically identify and eliminate:

    A. Defects

    B. Carbohydrates

    C. Waste

    D. Variation

E.  All the above.

14.  The Toyota's Total Production System (TPS) is synonymous with Lean Production. It is a methodology developed at Toyota under the guidance of:

A.  Yoko Ono

B.  John Lennon

C.  Taiichi Ohno

D.  Hiroshima

E.  Sakichi Toyoda

15.  The philosophy of TPS is that all process activities can be divided into either adding value or creating waste (muda).

A.  True

B.  False

16.  What famous author wrote: "Quality in a product or service is not what the supplier puts in. It is what the customer gets out and is willing to pay for. A product is not quality because it is hard to make and costs a lot of money, as manufacturers typically believe. This is incompetence. Customers pay only for what is of use to them and gives them value. Nothing else constitutes quality."

A.  Peter F. Drucker

B.  Jim Collins

C.  William J. Rothwell

D.  Wesley E. Donahue

E.  Henry Ford

17.  Joseph Juran said that "At least ___% of problems are in systems – fewer than ___% are attributable to some particular individual or set of circumstances."

A.  95 / 5

B.  85 / 15

C.  75 / 25

D.  60 / 40

E.  50 / 50

18.  Which of the following are true?

A.  The most dangerous kind of waste is the waste we do not recognize

B.  If you don't look for waste, you may not see it

C. A good place to start is by identifying processes that are either problematic or frustrating to you or others in your organization

D. The goal of TPS is to maximize value by eliminating waste and is considered applicable to any process

E. All are true

19. Which of the following are NOT common types of waste (muda) found in many organizations?

A. Unnecessary Inventory

B. Waiting

C. Excess Motion

D. Extra money

E. Over Processing

20. Underutilized Intellect may include:

A. Untapped skills - not asking people who do the job for input

B. Underutilizing employee skills and abilities

C. Using antiquated business tools and systems

D. Limited employee empowerment

E. All the above

21. Waiting is a major category of waste in many processes and may include:

A. Approvals from others – next operation waiting.

B. Information from others.

C. Equipment or systems downtime and unplanned interruptions that occur due to inefficiencies.

D. Delays due to scheduling of people or needed resources.

E. All the above.

**Answer**: E. All the above.

22. By definition, the Voice of the Customer (VOC) includes:

A. Customer demands.

B. Expectations.

C. Preferences.

D. Aversions.

E. All the above.

23. QFD helps transform customer needs (the Voice of the Customer) into:

A. Proposals that can be submitted to customers.

B. Technical characteristics for a product or service and prioritizing each product or service characteristic while simultaneously setting development targets for the product or service.

C. A Bill of Materials from which a product can be made.

D. A set of requirements used for the terms and conditions of purchase.

E. The legal requirements governing the contract language for a product or service.

24. The primary focus of employees of organizations should be trying to satisfy:

A. Their boss

B. The customer

C. Co-workers

D. Their friends

E. None of the above

## Concept 3 – Observe Processes and Scope Improvement Initiatives

25. Observation of process value streams (or lack thereof, waste) and questioning the status quo of an actual process (Gemba) are initial components for continuous process improvement. The term value stream is used in both Lean Sigma and Six Sigma as a descriptor of:

A. The value of people involved in the process.

B. The amount or stream of money required to develop an efficient process.

C. The necessary factors that contribute to the value of a product or service from the viewpoint of the customer.

D. The cost of the components of a process.

E. The benefits achieved for a Lean or Six Sigma intervention.

26. Observation of a process is a powerful, yet simple tool, and variations, along with their root causes, are major enemies.

A. True

B. False

27. Which of these are basic questions to ask when establishing the initial scope of the process being observed?

A. How much will it cost?

B. Where does the process begin and end?

C. Who should be involved?

D. What will happen if we do not accomplish anything?

E. What are the politics of the situation?

28. A typical project scope statement (or charter) contains the following information:

   A. Project title

   B. Project participants and stakeholders

   C. Description of project

   D. Why selected and who will sponsor or approve

   E. All the above

29. To be termed scientific, a method of inquiry must be based on gathering observable and measurable evidence.

   A. True

   B. False

30. When observing a process, what would you consider measuring?

   A. Wait time

   B. Excess Motion

   C. Extra processing or inventory

   D. Scrap and rework

   E. All the above

   **Answer**: E. All the above.

31. There are four basic rules associated with applying Toyota's Total Production System (TPS) or Lean Methodology to process improvement. The first rule is that all work shall be specified as to:

   A. Content

   B. Timing

   C. Outcome

   D. All the above

   E. None of the above

32. The second rule associated with applying Toyota's Total Production System (TPS) or Lean Methodology to process improvement is that:

   A. All work shall be specified as to content, sequence, timing, and outcome.

B. Every customer-supplier connection must be direct, and there must be an unambiguous yes-or-no way to send requests and receive responses.

C. The pathway for every product and service must be simple and direct

D. Any improvement must be made in accordance with the scientific method, under the guidance of an instructor, at the lowest possible level in the organization.

E. All processes are equal and should receive the same level of attention.

33. Which one of the following is NOT one of the four basic rules associated with applying Toyota's Total Production System (TPS)?

   A. All work shall be specified as to content, sequence, timing, and outcome.

   B. Every customer-supplier connection must be direct, and there must be an unambiguous yes-or-no way to send requests and receive responses.

   C. The pathway for every product and service must be simple and direct.

   D. Any improvement must be made in accordance with the scientific method, under the guidance of an instructor, at the lowest possible level in the organization.

   E. All processes are equal and should receive the same level of attention.

34. In engineering and project management, "niceties" and "extras" added to a project (often referred to as Gold-Plating) but not specified in the contract scope of work, is typically considered waste if the customer is not willing to pay for them.

   A. True

   B. False

35. A mistake often made by teams trying to implement Lean for the first time is:

   A. Asking fiends to join the team

   B. Not narrowing the scope of the process review and improvement initiative to something reasonable and doable

   C. Hiring a consultant

   D. Asking the boss for the budget and release time

   E. All the above

36. Observing processes and scoping potential process improvement initiatives is the responsibility of and should only be conducted by top management.

   A. True

   B. False

## Concept 4 – Diagram Processes Using Flowcharts and Process Maps

37. A flowchart or process map is a diagram that represents a process with the steps as boxes of various kinds and their order connected with arrows.

    A. True
    B. False

38. A flowchart or process map is a diagram that visually describes:

    A. Customer demand
    B. The cost of goods or services
    C. The flow of activities of the process
    D. The process steps in comparison with the ideal flow
    E. All the above

39. Which of the following are some process analysis, flowcharting, and process mapping activity considerations?

    A. Reflect on the voice of the customer(s), their expectations, and the steps in the process that either add-value or are problematic.
    B. Review each process step and consider the financial impact and the need for improvement.
    C. Consider the supply or value chain important to successfully completing each process step.
    D. All the above.
    E. None of the above.

40. When flowcharting an existing process it is best to initially focus on the sequence of how the ideal process should be.

    A. True
    B. False

41. A SIPOC diagram is a tool used to identify relevant components or key elements of a process improvement initiative. Which descriptor is NOT correct?

    A. S – Suppliers
    B. I – Improvement
    C. P – Process
    D. O – Outputs
    E. C – Customers

42. The starting point for developing a SIPOC is identifying:

    A. Customers

    B. Outputs

    C. Primary process steps

    D. Inputs

    E. Suppliers

43. The process SIPOC is often referred to as:

    A. A detailed picture of the process and stakeholders

    B. A high-level process map used to obtain a description of the process at hand, as well as define the boundaries of the project

    C. A tool for communicating project outcomes

    D. A map of process subcomponents

    E. None of the above

44. An overarching purpose for developing a SIPOC diagram is to:

    A. Provide a detailed roadmap of the process steps

    B. Graphically illustrate the process components and stakeholders as a method of better communicating the overall scope and complexity of a particular improvement initiative

    C. Provide a basis of process comparison

    D. Establish roles and functions of team members

    E. Develop metrics for improvement

45. A focus of the Toyota philosophy is keeping things simple.

    A. True

    B. False

    **Answer**: A. True.

46. For Lean it is important to focus on initiatives that are:

    A. Complicated and requires special expertise

    B. Projects where outside assistance is required

    C. Doable within a reasonable period of time

    D. Outside of your span of control or your team's span of control

    E. All the above

47. For Lean initiatives it is wise to start with improving the smaller processes that will have the most impact on your organization upon completion.

    A. True
    B. False

48. Process improvement initiatives within organizations can often be:

    A. Overwhelming
    B. Political
    C. Bureaucratic
    D. Complex
    E. All the above

## Concept 5 – Collect Data on Value Streams

49. Simply defined, a Value Stream Map (VSM) is a:

    A. Flowchart with metrics
    B. Diagram of a small creek
    C. Process map with metrics
    D. Both A and C
    E. None of the above

50. The important metrics or measures often included in a VSM are:

    A. Time
    B. Number of defects
    C. Output
    D. Delays
    E. All the above

51. A VSM could be a view of a process from:

    A. 10,000 feet
    B. 1,000 feet
    C. One foot
    D. One inch
    E. All the above

52. From whatever view is selected of a process, a primary objective is to identify all major activities as either value-adding or non-value adding.

    A. True

    B. False

53. According to common Lean methodology, you should draw Value Stream Maps in pencil on 11" x 17" paper (A3) to:

    A. Comply with copyright laws

    B. Permit ease of copying

    C. Promote simplicity and ease of change

    D. Follow established standards

    E. Facilitate ease of filing

54. Common symbols are often used to represent various actions or activities; however, you are free to use other symbols if they work better for you and your organization.

    A. True

    B. False

55. The suggested way of drawing a VSM is to:

    A. Start with client/person making request in upper right-hand corner of VSM form.

    B. Add all the ways requests or transmissions are made across top (from right to left).

    C. Draw VSM process steps across the center of page starting at the left-hand side.

    D. Add process steps (from left to right) and finish with client/person having request satisfied.

    E. All the above.

56. A Saw-tooth diagram is typically inserted across the bottom section of the VSM with important metrics including delays and when nothing is happening.

    A. True

    B. False

57. The term Takt time refers to:

    A. The time it takes to takt the process.

    B. A calculation that compares the time available to do work divided by the customer demand requirements for a product or service.

C. The output and delay time of process performance.

D. The time it takes to complete a process cycle.

E. The time recorded on the taktometer.

58. Which definition is incorrect?

A. Mura – a Japanese word that describes unevenness in a process.

B. Mura – a Japanese word that describes the future process.

C. Muri – a word that refers to overburdening or relying too much on one part of a process.

D. Muri – a Japanese word that describes the ideal process.

E. B and D are incorrect.

59. Which definition is correct?

A. Gemba – is Japanese for the actual place or real place which in the context of Lean translates to the place where the actual work or process is in operation and should be observed.

B. Kanban – a visual system that typically uses cards or stickers to control and alert people when inventories or flow problems occur.

C. Poka-Yoke – Japanese word for mistake proofing.

D. All are correct.

E. None are correct.

60. The Japanese word Kaizen means:

A. Mistake proofing

B. Waste

C. Celebrate

D. Continuous improvement.

E. Errors

## Concept 6 – Understand the A3 Problem Solving Methodology

61. A3 is a paper size (11" x 17") and this paper size has been used for decades in what is called now A3 Problem Solving.

A. True

B. False

62. The Left Side of A3 problem solving process (or left side of paper) is typically devoted to:

    A. Documenting the history of the organization

    B. Providing resumes or credentials of stakeholders

    C. Describing the Current State of process analysis

    D. Describing the Future State of process analysis

    E. Documenting the Benefit-Cost project justification

63. The Right Side of A3 problem solving process (or right side of paper) is typically devoted to:

    A. Documenting the history of the organization

    B. Providing resumes or credentials of stakeholders

    C. Describing the Current State of process analysis

    D. Describing the Future State of process analysis

    E. Documenting the Benefit-Cost project justification

64. Clarifying an improvement goal or the purpose or objective, or defining the problem sounds easy, but it is not! It requires using both parts of the brain. Often people identify:

    A. Who is to blame

    B. Solutions based on impressions of the situation

    C. How people feel about a problem

    D. Symptoms of the problem and do not get to the root cause(s)

    E. All the above

65. Revolutionary problem-solving methodologies and tools are often used in Lean.

    A. True

    B. False

66. An observation worksheet may be one type of checklist.

    A. True

    B. False

67. Histograms are used to:

    A. Display density of data.

    B. Estimate the probability density function of the underlying variable.

    C. Treat a cold.

    D. A and B are correct.

    E. None are correct.

68. Which of the following are true or Pareto Charts?

    A. Named after Vilfredo Pareto, an Italian engineer and economist.

    B. This type of chart illustrates and represents individual values in descending order (typically bars).

    C. The cumulative total is represented by a line.

    D. The tool is particularly useful in determining which opportunities for improvement may be the best to start with.

    E. All are correct.

69. The Pareto Chart illustrates and represents individual values in descending order and the lowest valued item should be the focus of initial improvement analysis.

    A. True

    B. False

70. Surveys are merely a method for collecting quantitative information about items in a population.

    A. True

    B. False

71. A3 problem solving was institutionalized and popularized by:

    A. General Electric

    B. Motorola

    C. Toyota

    D. NASA

    E. Siemans

72. Which tool is NOT a traditional problem identification tool?

    A. Pareto Chart

    B. Surveys

    C. Check Sheet

    D. Gantt Chart

    E. Histogram

## Concept 7 – Apply Tools for Analyzing the Current Situation

73. Traditional brainstorming is a process improvement tool with rules. Which item is NOT one of the rules?

A. Focus on quantity

B. Withhold criticism

C. Welcome unusual ideas

D. Focus on quality

E. Combine and improve ideas

74. From experience, traditional brainstorming is an intense activity and after about how many minutes do many participants get easily distracted and disengage?

A. One minute

B. 5 to 10 minutes

C. 30 to 45 minutes

D. 60 to 90 minutes

E. 120 to 200 minutes

75. The causes of almost any problem can be placed into four major categories of a Cause and Effect diagram. Which item is NOT one of the traditional categories?

A. Manpower or people

B. Methods or procedures

C. Materials

D. Machinery or equipment

E. Money

76. To get to the Root Cause of almost any problem it is suggested you ask "Why" 5 times. Of course, you may get to the root by asking Why, or you could insert:

A. Who

B. What

C. Where

D. When

E. All the above

77. After you get to the Root Cause(s), the question(s) becomes:

A. What are you going to do about it?

B. What are practical actions or countermeasures that should be taken?

C. What are your realistic goals for improving the situation?

D. How would you know when you achieve your goals?

E. All the above.

78. A Cause and Effect Diagram is also called:

    A. Tree diagram
    B. Ishikawa diagram
    C. Fishbone diagram
    D. Woodshed diagram
    E. Both B. and C

79. A Cause and Effect Diagram is commonly used to identify:

    A. Potential factors causing an overall effect.
    B. Potential barriers or challenges to achieving the goal of having the best process.
    C. The person to blame for the situation.
    D. Potential money making schemes.
    E. Both A and b are correct.

80. A technique that allows a group to quickly prioritize many issues, concerns, and improvement ideas using a weighted ranking is:

    A. Force Field Analysis
    B. Nominal Group Technique
    C. Stratification
    D. Scatter Diagram
    E. Run Chart

81. A tool that can be thought of as a prioritized pro and con diagram whereby the Driving Forces (Pro) and the Restraining Forces (Con) associated with an event are often displayed in descending balance sheet "T-Account" format is called a:

    A. Force Field Analysis
    B. Nominal Group Technique
    C. Stratification
    D. Scatter Diagram
    E. Run Chart

82. A process of classifying data into subgroups or categories used for analyzing a listing of potential problem causes (or barriers and challenges) is called:

    A. Force Field Analysis
    B. Nominal Group Technique
    C. Stratification

    D. Scatter Diagram

    E. Run Chart

83. A graphical representation of data displayed in a time sequence, often to represent some aspect of the output or performance of a business process, is called a:

    A. Force Field Analysis

    B. Nominal Group Technique

    C. Stratification

    D. Scatter Diagram

    E. Run Chart

84. In what technique is data displayed as a collection of points, each having the value of one variable determining the position on the horizontal axis and the value of the other variable determining the position on the vertical axis?

    A. Force Field Analysis

    B. Nominal Group Technique

    C. Stratification

    D. Scatter Diagram or Plot

    E. Run Chart

## Concept 8 – Apply Tools for Future State Planning

85. Common tools used for Future State planning and completion of the right side of an A3 Problem Solving Form include:

    A. 5S Tools and Methodology

    B. Spaghetti Diagrams

    C. Standardized Work Plans

    D. Just In Time Inventory (JIT) planning

    E. All the above

86. The Future State plan should always be the same as the Ideal State.

    A. True

    B. False

87. Which is NOT one of the 5S's:

    A. Sort (seiri)

    B. Straighten (seiton)

C. Shine (seiso)

D. Synthesize (sysiketsu)

E. Sustain (shitsuke)

88. The first "S" in the 5S methodology is Sorting and it has guidelines. Which is NOT one of the guidelines?

    A. Take stock of inventory in work area.

    B. Get rid of all non-essential items.

    C. Keep regularly needed items in storage.

    D. Put less needed items further away or higher up.

    E. Free up storage space.

89. What are the kinds of questions do you need to ask about each item being sorted?

    A. Useable or not useable

    B. Essential, wanted, unwanted, current, or obsolete

    C. Used frequently or infrequently

    D. Better stored somewhere else

    E. All the above

90. Another S in the 5S methodology is Shine and it has guidelines. Which guidelines are correct?

    A. Clean the workspace.

    B. Make sure each piece of equipment is clean and in working order.

    C. Start with main work area and work out from there.

    D. All materials needed for work are available and marked.

    E. All are correct.

91. Sustaining is the last "S" in the 5S methodology. Which of the following is NOT a good idea to implement?

    A. Review the workplace regularly.

    B. Consider starting with "Standardize" each time a product change occurs and when new materials or forms are added to the inventory.

    C. Audit regularly and post the scores.

    D. Make plans and assignments for maintaining and improving the area.

92. Which of the following describes a Spaghetti Diagram?

A. Is a Point-to-Point diagram and an excellent way to demonstrate a Current or Future state or condition.

B. Graphic representation of employees, clients, materials, equipment, or information travel in a defined work area.

C. A pencil drawing on a layout diagram of the workspace.

D. All the above.

E. None of the above.

93. Standard Work is typically the most effective combination of people, materials, and equipment. Creating Standard Work Plans is a method whereby you typically focus on continuously improving the major categories or elements of the Cause and Effect diagram: people, materials, equipment, and methods, until the most effective or standard is achieved.

A. True

B. False

94. Sometimes countermeasures are needed to implement standard work plans or other future state implementation plans. A countermeasure may be thought of as:

A. Actions taken to prevent an undesirable event.

B. Actions to prevent undesirable outcomes.

C. Proactive actions to achieve your objectives.

D. All the above are true.

E. None of the above are true.

95. Which of the following elements are NOT typically included in the Right Side of an A3 Problem Solving Form or Analysis?

A. Future State Description or Map

B. Countermeasures

C. Description of the Problem

D. Implementation Plan and Benefit-Cost Analysis

E. Checks and Follow-Up Action

96. The tools used for Future State Planning can be deceptively difficult and costly to implement, and the results you obtain do not really matter.

A. True

B. False

## Concept 9 – Identify Tools for Six Sigma Quality

97.  Six Sigma may be described as:

 A.  A continuous improvement methodology that utilizes statistical concepts.

 B.  A methodology initially adopted by Motorola to reduce variation, eliminate defects, and perfect processes.

 C.  A top-down methodology that typically requires management support.

 D.  A methodology that requires commitment of people, time, and other resources.

 E.  All the above.

98.  Six Sigma is a statistical measurement (6 σ) meaning six standard deviations between the process mean and the nearest specification limit.

 A.  True

 B.  False

99.  If a process can produce products or services at a one sigma quality level, what per cent of the products or services would be defect free?

 A.  68.26%

 B.  95.44%

 C.  99.73%

 D.  99.99%

 E.  None of the above

100.  If a process can produce products or services at a six sigma quality level, what per cent of the products or services would be defect free?

 A.  68.26%

 B.  95.44%

 C.  99.73%

 D.  99.99%

 E.  None of the above

101.  Six Sigma is a business philosophy, strategy, methodology and threshold of excellence originally developed by Motorola in the 1970's and often characterized by its use of belts. Which of the following are correct?

 A.  Champions – Senior management: Leaders responsible for the success of Six Sigma efforts.

B. Black Belts – Leaders of teams responsible for measuring, analyzing, improving, and controlling processes that influence customer satisfaction and productivity growth. Black Belts also hold full-time positions.

C. Green Belts – Green Belts are trained by a similar method as Black Belts but usually stay in their operating assignments, working Six Sigma projects part-time, typically as team leaders.

D. Yellow Belts - Are typically team members or others associated in some way with Six

E. Sigma projects. As such, they support the goals of the project usually in the context of their existing responsibilities. They must understand the overall concepts and terminology of Six Sigma.

F. All are correct.

102. Which is NOT one of the five steps for the DMAIC process, synonymous with the process for achieving Six Sigma quality?

    A. Define
    B. Measure
    C. Analyze
    D. Implement
    E. Control

103. Statistical control charts and statistical process control (SPC) methodologies are sometimes used to monitor the stability and quality of a process as an aid in maintaining statistical control. A process or any operation is said to be in a state of statistical control if, from the evidence gathered in a sample, it can be deuced or inferred with a high degree of confidence that the process or operation is behaving in a way other than it should be performing.

    A. True
    B. False

104. The consistency of a process or ability of a process to meet its purpose is often referred to as process capability. All processes have inherent statistical variability that can be evaluated by statistical methods. Which software package is widely used to help simplify the calculations associated with process capability studies and other Lean statistical analysis needs?

    A. Microsoft Project
    B. IBM - Statistical Package for the Social Sciences (SPSS)
    C. AutoDeskSys -Form Z
    D. MiniTab

E. Statistical Lab

105. Hypothesis Testing / Confidence Intervals is used as a method of making data driven decisions with the purpose of:

 A. Proving the null hypothesis

 B. Determining the level of no-confidence

 C. Determining the level of statistical significance

 D. Disproving the null hypothesis

 E. All the above

106. Analysis of Variance (ANOVA) / Parametric Tests are used to compare:

 A. The paranormal event

 B. The paranormal equation

 C. The parametric situation

 D. The variances of selected events

 E. None of the above

107. Correlation and Regression Analysis are used to determine the strength of data:

 A. Similarities

 B. Variance

 C. Negativity

 D. Relationships

 E. Divergence

108. Reliability Estimates and Tolerancing Techniques typically refers to:

 A. The consistency of a measure

 B. The amount of similarity

 C. The divergence estimate

 D. All the above

 E. None of the above

## Concept 10 – Prepare Initiative Justifications and Reports

109. Which of the following are potential benefits of pursuing Lean-initiatives?

 A. Improved cash flow

 B. Reduced inventory

 C. Improved quality

D. Reduced waste

E. All the above are potential benefits of Lean initiatives

110. When planning a presentation, you need to consider which of the following:

A. Who will be attending

B. How much time you have to present

C. The location

D. What might go wrong

E. All the above

111. When presenting the results of a Lean initiative, identify WIIFM; which stands for the acronym:

A. What's In It For Many

B. What's In It For Money

C. What's In It For Me

D. What's In It For Mary

E. None of the above

112. When presenting, remember the adage that a picture is worth:

A. A million words

B. A thousand words

C. A hundred words

D. A zillion words

E. A billion words

113. For typical Lean projects, a 10-minute presentation to present the summary findings and recommendations followed by a discussion period of 5 to 10 minutes would be appropriate.

A. True

B. False

114. Assertion-evidence based presentation slides typically start with a sentence headline that states the main assertion of the slide. That headline assertion is then supported by a:

A. Bullet list of statements

B. Outline of key components

C. Visual evidence

D. Detailed data

E. Testimonials

115. For a Lean presentation, which element should NOT be included when describing the Current Situation (Left Side of A3):

A. Issue or problem

B. Countermeasures

C. Background and Costs

D. Value Stream Map

E. Goals and Targets

116. For a Lean presentation, which element should NOT be included when describing the Future Situation (Right Side of A3):

A. Control charts

B. Countermeasures

C. Implementation plan

D. Benefits and costs and Return on Investment (ROI)

E. Lessons learned

117. The content of a Lean presentation should address the impact of pursuing a Lean initiative. Typically, this requires gathering information on the costs and benefits. Return on Investment equals the benefits divided by the costs.

A. True

B. False

118. An improvement project that costs more than the anticipated benefits is a good one to pursue.

A. True

B. False

119. The lessons learned may include which of the following:

A. Review of the initial scope statement (or project charter) to determine if all elements were addressed

B. Description of which tools were most useful

C. Comments on how the initiative is perceived in the workplace

D. Discussion of the impact

E. All the above

120. Regardless of your position in an organization, waste and defects can be a concern and sooner or later you may be expected to participate in a continuous

improvement activity or project. Knowing the language of Lean Sigma, Six Sigma, and other continuous improvement methodologies and how to select and apply various tools and techniques can be of value. Which of the following are true of Lean?

A. The basic principles of Lean are the identification and elimination of waste throughout the organization; the basic principles of Six Sigma are to reduce variation and defects

B. Much of the waste and process variation in organizations is problematic because management and employees may accept them as necessary

C. Lean is an ongoing, team-based effort of continuous improvement for many organizations

D. Lean initiatives are customer-driven

E. All the above

# Lean Six Sigma Process Improvement Yellow Belt – Practice Test - Correct Answers

| Concept 1 | | Concept 2 | | Concept 3 | | Concept 4 | | Concept 5 | |
|---|---|---|---|---|---|---|---|---|---|
| 1. | E | 13. | C | 25. | C | 37. | A | 49. | D |
| 2. | D | 14. | C | 26. | A | 38. | C | 50. | E |
| 3. | B | 15. | A | 27. | B | 39. | D | 51. | E |
| 4. | B | 16. | A | 28. | E | 40. | B | 52. | A |
| 5. | A | 17. | B | 29. | A | 41. | B | 53. | C |
| 6. | A | 18. | E | 30. | E | 42. | C | 54. | A |
| 7. | D | 19. | D | 31. | D | 43. | B | 55. | E |
| 8. | C | 20. | E | 32. | B | 44. | B | 56. | A |
| 9. | A | 21. | E | 33. | E | 45. | A | 57. | B |
| 10. | C | 22. | E | 34. | A | 46. | C | 58. | E |
| 11. | E | 23. | B | 35. | B | 47. | A | 59. | D |
| 12. | B | 24. | B | 36. | B | 48. | E | 60. | D |

| Concept 6 | | Concept 7 | | Concept 8 | | Concept 9 | | Concept 10 | |
|---|---|---|---|---|---|---|---|---|---|
| 61. | A | 73. | D | 85. | E | 97. | E | 109. | E |
| 62. | C | 74. | B | 86. | B | 98. | A | 110. | E |
| 63. | D | 75. | E | 87. | D | 99. | A | 111. | C |
| 64. | E | 76. | E | 88. | C | 100. | D | 112. | B |
| 65. | B | 77. | E | 89. | E | 101. | E | 113. | A |
| 66. | A | 78. | E | 90. | E | 102. | D | 114. | C |
| 67. | D | 79. | E | 91. | B | 103. | B | 115. | B |
| 68. | E | 80. | B | 92. | D | 104. | D | 116. | A |
| 69. | B | 81. | A | 93. | A | 105. | C | 117. | A |
| 70. | B | 82. | C | 94. | D | 106. | D | 118. | B |
| 71. | C | 83. | E | 95. | C | 107. | D | 119. | E |
| 72. | D | 84. | D | 96. | B | 108. | A | 120. | E |

*I never dreamed about success. I worked for it.*

– Estee Lauder

# Appendices: Lean Six Sigma Worksheets

These appendices provide worksheets for the following Lean tools:

**Appendix A**: Lean Six Sigma Project Scope Statement Worksheet

**Appendix B**: Observation Worksheet

**Appendix C**: SIPOC Worksheet

**Appendix D**: Value Stream Map Worksheet

**Appendix E**: A3 Problem Solving Worksheet

**Appendix F**: Brainstorming Worksheet

**Appendix G**: Cause and Effect Diagram Worksheet

**Appendix H**: 5S Assessment Worksheet

**Appendix I**: Standard Work Plan Worksheet

**Appendix J**: Risk Analysis and Planning Audit (RAPA) Worksheet

**Appendix K**: Lean Six Sigma Tools Checklist

## Appendix A. Lean Six Sigma Project Scope Statement Worksheet

Work Process:

_____

_____

_____

Participants:

_____

_____

_____

_____

Process Description (include beginning and end points):

_____

_____

_____

_____

_____

_____

_____

_____

Why Selected:

_____

_____

Objectives:

_____

_____

Sponsor:

_____

_____

# Appendix B. Observation Worksheet

OBSERVATION WORKSHEET

| Process: _____ | Layout of Work Area |
|---|---|
| Person Observed: _____ | |
| Location: _____ | |
| Observer: _____ | |
| Date: _____ | |
| Start Time: _____ Finish: _____ | |

| Times | Activity | UNDERUTILIZED INTELLECT | WAITING | EXCESS MOTION | EXTRA PROCESSING | OVER PRODUCING | UNNECESSARY INVENTORY | TRANSPORTATION | CORRECTIONS, REWORK & SCRAP | OTHER: | Notes |
|---|---|---|---|---|---|---|---|---|---|---|---|
| : : | | | | | | | | | | | |
| : : | | | | | | | | | | | |
| : : | | | | | | | | | | | |
| : : | | | | | | | | | | | |
| : : | | | | | | | | | | | |
| : : | | | | | | | | | | | |
| : : | | | | | | | | | | | |
| : : | | | | | | | | | | | |
| : : | | | | | | | | | | | |
| : : | | | | | | | | | | | |
| : : | | | | | | | | | | | |
| : : | | | | | | | | | | | |
| : : | | | | | | | | | | | |
| : : | | | | | | | | | | | |
| : : | | | | | | | | | | | |
| : : | | | | | | | | | | | |
| : : | | | | | | | | | | | |
| : : | | | | | | | | | | | |
| : : | | | | | | | | | | | |
| : : | | | | | | | | | | | |
| : : | | | | | | | | | | | |
| : : | | | | | | | | | | | |

## Appendix C. SIPOC Worksheet

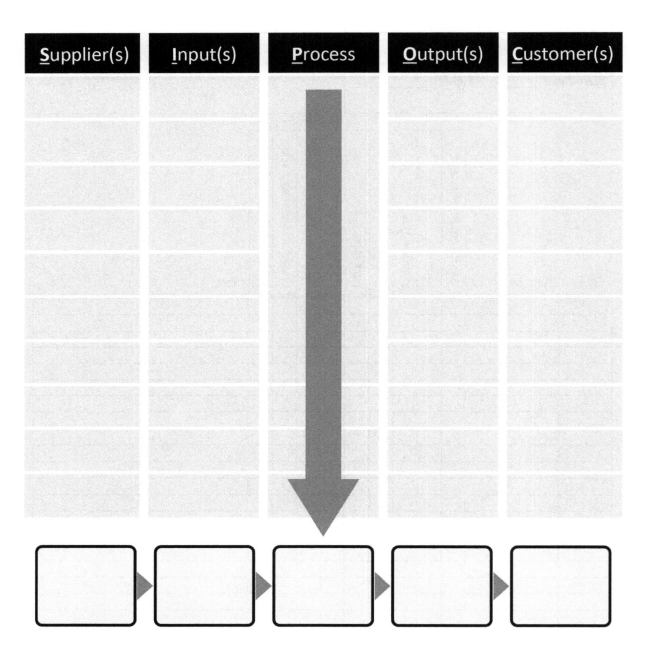

| SIPOC for: _____ | Team members:_____ _____ | Date: _____ |

| **S**upplier(s) | **I**nput(s) | **P**rocess | **O**utput(s) | **C**ustomer(s) |
| --- | --- | --- | --- | --- |

**Process Steps**

# Appendix D. Value Stream Map Worksheet

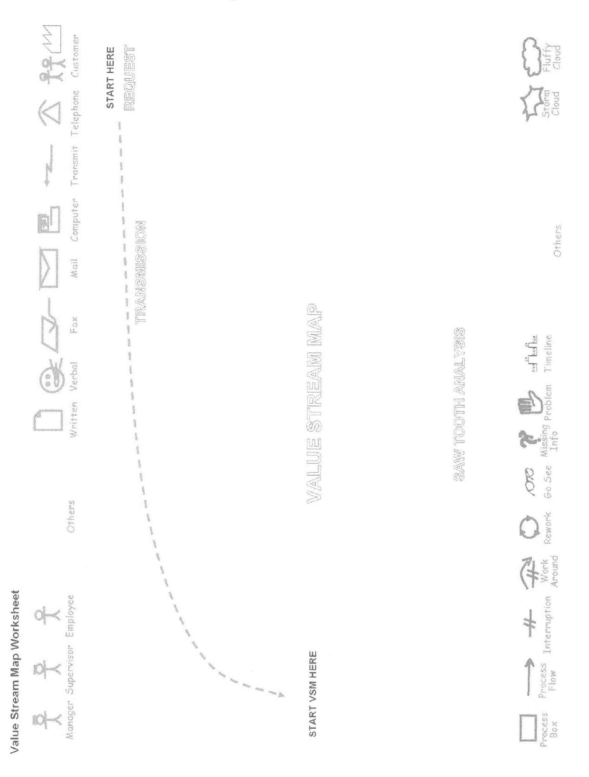

## Appendix D. Value Stream Map Worksheet (11x17 view)

### Value Stream Map Worksheet

Manager  Supervisor  Employee   Others   Written  Ve

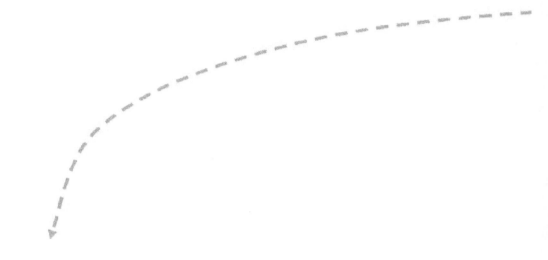

START VSM HERE

VALUE STRE

SAW TOOTH A

Process   Process   Interruption   Work    Rework   Go See   Missing  Problem
Box       Flow                     Around                     Info

rbal     Fax     Mail     Computer     Transmit     Telephone     Customer

**START HERE**

REQUEST

TRANSMISSION

AM MAP

NALYSIS

Timeline

Others

Storm
Cloud

Fluffy
Cloud

## Appendix E. A3 Problem Solving Worksheet (11x17 view)

ISSUE:

BACKGROUND AND COSTS:

CURRENT STATE:

SITUATION ANALYSIS:

GOALS AND TARGET:

**FUTURE STATE:**

TITLE: _____

To: _____

BY: _____

DATE: _____

**COUNTERMEASURES:**

_____
_____
_____
_____
_____
_____
_____
_____

**IMPLEMENTATION PLAN:**

| WHAT | WHO | WHEN | DONE? |
|------|-----|------|-------|
|  |  |  |  |
|  |  |  |  |
|  |  |  |  |
|  |  |  |  |
|  |  |  |  |
|  |  |  |  |

| **IMPLEMENTATION COST** | **IMPLEMENTATION BENEFITS** |
|-------------------------|------------------------------|
|  |  |
|  |  |
|  |  |
|  |  |

**CHECK:**

_____
_____

| **FOLLOW UP ACTIONS** | WHO | WHEN | DONE? |
|-----------------------|-----|------|-------|
|  |  |  |  |
|  |  |  |  |
|  |  |  |  |
|  |  |  |  |

# Appendix E. A3 Problem Solving Worksheet

TITLE: _____

TO: _____
BY: _____
DATE: _____

ISSUE:

BACKGROUND AND COSTS:

CURRENT STATE:

FUTURE STATE:

SITUATION ANALYSIS:

COUNTERMEASURES:

IMPLEMENTATION PLAN:

| WHAT | WHO | WHEN | DONE? |
|------|-----|------|-------|
|      |     |      |       |

IMPLEMENTATION COST

IMPLEMENTATION BENEFITS

CHECK:

GOALS AND TARGET:

FOLLOW UP ACTIONS

| | WHO | WHEN | DONE? |
|--|-----|------|-------|
|  |     |      |       |

## Appendix F. Brainstorming Worksheet

| Category? | Barriers and Challenges |
|---|---|
| | 1. |
| | 2. |
| | 3. |
| | 4. |
| | 5. |
| | 6. |
| | 7. |
| | 8. |
| | 9. |
| | 10. |
| | 11. |
| | 12. |
| | 13. |
| | 14. |
| | 15. |
| | 16. |
| | 17. |
| | 18. |
| | 19. |
| | 20. |
| | 21. |
| | 22. |
| | 23. |
| | 24. |
| | 25. |

## Appendix G. Cause and Effect Diagram Worksheet

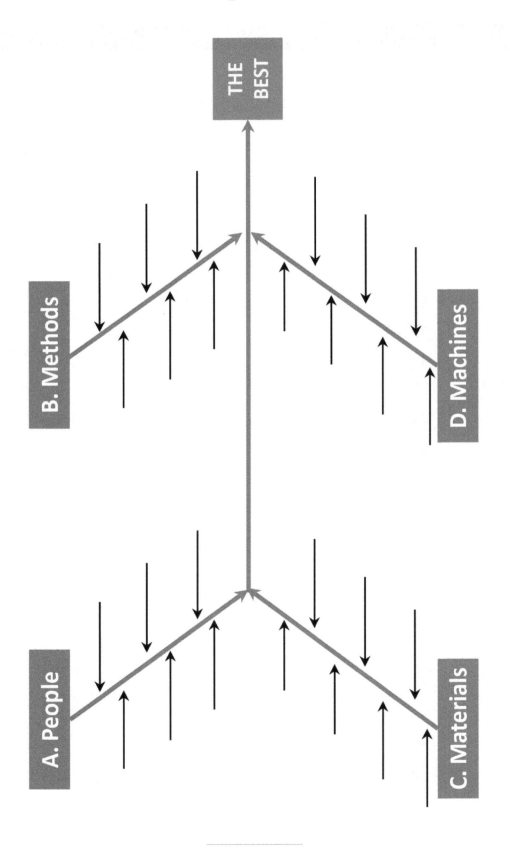

## Appendix H. 5S Assessment Worksheet

# 5S Assessment

Organization / Work Area: _____

By: _____   Date: _____

*Instructions*: Next to each statement, check the number (1 to 5) that indicates your level of agreement with the statement, with **1** being **strongly disagree** and **5** being **strongly agree**. When finished total your ratings.

| | | | 1 | 2 | 3 | 4 | 5 |
|---|---|---|---|---|---|---|---|
| **SORT** (Seiri) | | Procedures are established and evident. Every item in the area is needed for regular work. No extraneous items are found in any area location. Only the minimum standard amount of inventory and supplies are in the area. | | | | | |
| **STRAIGHTEN** (Seiton) | | All items have a specific location and in their proper place. Area is very well organized with regularly used items stored in designated convenient locations. Excellent visual controls are in evidence. | | | | | |
| **SHINE** (Seiso) | | Equipment, work surfaces and storage areas are clean. Every item in the area is in "like new" condition. The area is thoroughly cleaned on a regular basis and is kept in a spotless condition. | | | | | |
| **STANDARDIZE** (Seiketsu) | | Specific organizing tasks have been assigned for the work area with responsibilities clearly noted. There is an up-to-work area layout diagram, duty list, and schedule posted. There is evidence that duties are done regularly. | | | | | |
| **SUSTAIN** (Shitsuke) | | Everyone is involved in improvement activities and all levels of the organization are dedicated to sustaining the 5S program. There is regular leadership participation in reviews. All areas are "audit ready" at all times. | | | | | |
| | | **TOTAL RATING (Add Values)** | | | | | |

## Appendix I. Standard Work Plan Worksheet

Process or Sub-Process: _____

Layout of Work Area

| Work Elements | | TIME | | | Minutes | | | | | | | | | |
|---|---|---|---|---|---|---|---|---|---|---|---|---|---|---|
| Task # | Description | Work | Travel | Wait | 1 | 2 | 3 | 4 | 5 | 6 | 7 | 8 | 9 | 10 |
| | | | | | | | | | | | | | | |
| | | | | | | | | | | | | | | |
| | | | | | | | | | | | | | | |
| | | | | | | | | | | | | | | |
| | | | | | | | | | | | | | | |
| | | | | | | | | | | | | | | |
| | | | | | | | | | | | | | | |
| | | | | | | | | | | | | | | |
| | | | | | | | | | | | | | | |
| | | | | | | | | | | | | | | |
| | | | | | | | | | | | | | | |
| | | | | | | | | | | | | | | |
| | | | | | | | | | | | | | | |
| | | | | | | | | | | | | | | |
| | | | | | | | | | | | | | | |
| | | | | | | | | | | | | | | |
| | | | | | | | | | | | | | | |
| | | | | | | | | | | | | | | |
| | | | | | | | | | | | | | | |
| | | | | | | | | | | | | | | |
| | | | | | | | | | | | | | | |
| | | | | | | | | | | | | | | |
| | | | | | | | | | | | | | | |
| | | | | | | | | | | | | | | |

## Appendix J. Risk Analysis and Planning Audit (RAPA) Worksheet

| Ref. # | A. Key Project Activities | B. Potential Adverse Events | C. Potential Cause of Adverse Event(s) | D. Potential Effects of Adverse Event(s) on the Project and Customer | E. Severity (1-5) | F. Estimated Impact in Time and Money | G. Likelihood (1-5) | H. Recommended Actions to Eliminate or Enhance Prevention or Detection | I. Effectiveness (1-5) | J. Risk Priority Number (RPN) | K. Responsibility for Action Accepted by | L. What Actions Can You Take If It Does Occur? | M. Action Priority (A-E) |
|---|---|---|---|---|---|---|---|---|---|---|---|---|---|
| 1 | | | | | | | | | | | | | |
| 2 | | | | | | | | | | | | | |
| 3 | | | | | | | | | | | | | |
| 4 | | | | | | | | | | | | | |
| 5 | | | | | | | | | | | | | |
| 6 | | | | | | | | | | | | | |
| 7 | | | | | | | | | | | | | |
| 8 | | | | | | | | | | | | | |
| 9 | | | | | | | | | | | | | |
| 10 | | | | | | | | | | | | | |
| 11 | | | | | | | | | | | | | |
| 12 | | | | | | | | | | | | | |
| 13 | | | | | | | | | | | | | |
| 14 | | | | | | | | | | | | | |
| 15 | | | | | | | | | | | | | |

## Appendix J. Risk Analysis and Planning Audit (RAPA) Worksheet (11x17 view)

| Ref. # | A. Key Project Activities | B. Potential Adverse Events | C. Potential Cause of Adverse Event(s) | D. Potential Effects of Adverse Event(s) on the Project and Customer | E. Severity (1-5) | F. Estimated Impact in Time and Money |
|--------|---------------------------|-----------------------------|----------------------------------------|---------------------------------------------------------------------|-------------------|----------------------------------------|
| 1 | | | | | | |
| 2 | | | | | | |
| 3 | | | | | | |
| 4 | | | | | | |
| 5 | | | | | | |
| 6 | | | | | | |
| 7 | | | | | | |
| 8 | | | | | | |
| 9 | | | | | | |
| 10 | | | | | | |
| 11 | | | | | | |
| 12 | | | | | | |
| 13 | | | | | | |
| 14 | | | | | | |
| 15 | | | | | | |

| G. | H. | I. | J. | K. | L. | M. |
|----|----|----|----|----|----|----|
| Likelihood (1-5) | Recommended Actions to Eliminate or Enhance Prevention or Detection | Effectiveness (1-5) | Risk Priority Number (RPN) | Responsibility for Action Accepted by | What Actions Can You Take If It Does Occur? | Action Priority (A-E) |
| | | | | | | |
| | | | | | | |
| | | | | | | |
| | | | | | | |
| | | | | | | |
| | | | | | | |
| | | | | | | |
| | | | | | | |
| | | | | | | |

## Appendix K. Lean Six Sigma Tools Checklist

### Current State and Situation Analysis

- ☐ Project Scope or Charter Statement
- ☐ Flowchart or Process Map
- ☐ Value Stream Map (Current State)
- ☐ Data Collection Plan and Sampling (data reported in Value Stream Map)
- ☐ Observation Data Worksheets and Charts
- ☐ SIPOC Diagram (Suppliers, Inputs, Process, Outputs, Customers)
- ☐ Structured Brainstorming
- ☐ Cause and Effect Diagram and Matrix
- ☐ Pareto Diagram and Analysis (most important issues from customer's perspective)
- ☐ Run Charts and Control Charts
- ☐ Capabilities Studies
- ☐ QFD Diagram (Quality, Function, Deployment)
- ☐ Root Cause Analysis (5 Whys)
- ☐ Hypothesis Testing and Confidence Intervals
- ☐ Analysis of Variance (ANOVA) and Parametric Tests
- ☐ Correlation and Regression Analysis
- ☐ Reliability Estimates and Tolerancing Techniques

### Future State and Implementation

- ☐ A3 Problem Solving Worksheet and Gap Analysis
- ☐ Spaghetti Charts
- ☐ Cellular – Modular Flow Diagram
- ☐ Workplace Organization and 5S Tools (Sort, Straighten, Scrub, Standardize, Sustain)
- ☐ Just in Time (JIT)
- ☐ Quick Changeover and Set-Up Reduction
- ☐ Pull and Kanban (Visible Record)
- ☐ Countermeasures and Poka-Yoke (mistake proofing)
- ☐ Visual Management
- ☐ Total Productive Maintenance (TPM)
- ☐ Design of Experiments (DOE)
- ☐ Failure Mode Effect Analysis (FMEA)
- ☐ Risk Analysis and Planning Audit (RAPA)
- ☐ Implementation Plan (Who, What, Where, When, Why, How)
- ☐ Pilot Testing
- ☐ Dashboard Metrics and Cost-Benefit Analysis
- ☐ Monitoring Plan and Follow-up Actions
- ☐ Lessons Learned

# Index

## A

## B

## C

# P

# Q

# R

# About the Author

## Wesley E. Donahue, PhD, PE, PLS, PMP®, 6σ Blackbelt

As a business owner, engineer, manager, and now an educator, I have always thought of myself as being in the business of helping other people succeed. But like you, at each step of the way I had to learn, and I had to put that learning into action. My latest book *Unlocking Lean Six Sigma – A Competency-Based Approach to Applying Continuous Process Improvement Principles and Best Practices* speaks from the voice of experience.

As for my background, I am a professor of Organization Development at Penn State University. In this capacity, I am engaged in top-ranked graduate research and programming in learning and performance systems and lead a successful online graduate program in organization development and change. I am also president of Centrestar, Inc. a firm that offers a unique and straightforward approach for professionals to assess their leadership skills, develop personalized roadmaps for success, and access on-demand micro-learning courses that get results. View our courses at: www.centrestar.com

Before that, I was Director of Penn State Management Development Programs and Services, where I provided education and training services to business and industry clients around the world. Prior to that, I had years of experience as a manager, leader, and business owner. I was regional sales vice-president for a mid-sized plasics packaging manfacturer; co-founder and executive vice-president of a manufacturing company; corporate and international manager of technology for a *Fortune 200* multi-national company; and I also co-owned and operated a retail business.

I am a registered professional engineer and land surveyor with an MBA, Six Sigma black belt, certified project management professional (PMP®), co-author of *Creating In-house Sales Training and Development Programs*, and author of *Building Leadership Competence*, as well as a host of short courses and other education and training materials.

I would enjoy hearing from you and finding out how this book has helped you achieve your goals. Please contact me at wdonahue@centrestar.com

Best wishes for your continued success.

CPSIA information can be obtained
at www.ICGtesting.com
Printed in the USA
BVHW010505100922
646721BV00004BA/60